To dear Brian –

With my warmest wishes
upon your retirement,
and for its attendant
emancipation –
from where it all began –

Philip .

June 2004 .

A SHORT HISTORY OF THE

UNIVERSITY of MELBOURNE

A SHORT HISTORY OF THE

UNIVERSITY of MELBOURNE

STUART MACINTYRE and R. J. W. SELLECK

MELBOURNE UNIVERSITY PRESS

THE UNIVERSITY OF
MELBOURNE
1853–2003
150
YEARS

MELBOURNE UNIVERSITY PRESS
An imprint of Melbourne University Publishing (MUP Ltd)
PO Box 1167, Carlton, Victoria 3053, Australia
mup-info@unimelb.edu.au
www.mup.com.au

First published 2003
Text ©Stuart Macintyre and Richard Selleck 2003
Design and typography © Melbourne University Publishing (MUP Ltd) 2003

Typeset in 10 point Elegant Garamond by Alice Graphics
Printed in Australia by BPA Print Group

National Library of Australia Cataloguing-in-Publication entry

Macintyre, Stuart, 1947- .
    A short history of the University of Melbourne.

    Bibliography.
    Includes index.
    ISBN 0 522 85058 8.

    1. University of Melbourne—History. 2. Universities and colleges—Victoria—Melbourne—History. 3. Education, Higher—Victoria—Melbourne—History. I. Selleck, R. J. W. (Richard Joseph Wheeler), 1934– . II. Title.
378.9451

Contents

As It Was in the Beginning

When teaching began at the University of Melbourne on 13 April 1855 three professors faced sixteen students; the university's governing body, its Council, was more numerous. Five students, including Caroline Chisholm's son Archibald, left without completing a subject; two (Henry Wrixon, later a vice-chancellor, and his brother) studied for two years then abandoned Melbourne for Trinity College, Dublin; and Joseph Proctor Bainbridge, whose son was to become the university's registrar, dropped out after a year. Three of the four who abandoned their studies most swiftly came from St Francis Seminary, where they were training to be priests. Only four of the original sixteen graduated.

The slow start dampened the hope which had accompanied the university's establishment. An Act of Incorporation was passed in January 1853, driven partly by a desire to match the university that Sydney had opened the previous year. The city's professionals (merchants, government officers, civil servants, politicians, lawyers, doctors and clergymen) created the demand for the university and dominated its Council, which was appointed in April by Lieutenant-Governor Charles La Trobe.

Under the thrusting leadership of its Chancellor, the Supreme Court judge Redmond Barry, the university secured land one mile north of the city in Carlton, appointed a registrar to keep the records and administer its affairs, and selected the first professors through a committee set up in London. A

The east and north wings of the Quadrangle, *c.*1865, which was built by immigrants to summon memories of the country they had left.

Tudor Gothic quadrangle designed by Francis White (only three sides were finished) evoked memories of ancient British universities and eventually housed the professors and their families as well as the classrooms and lecture-theatres in which the professors taught. The Professor of Classics died soon after his arrival and, while a replacement was sought, the founding professors, Frederick McCoy (natural science), William Wilson (mathematics and natural philosophy—physics in today's terms) and William Hearn (modern history and literature, political economy and logic) began teaching.

On the foundation stone, which has somehow been lost, Barry had placed a declaration that the university was 'instituted in honour of God, for establishing young men in philosophy, literature and piety, cultivating the talent of youth, fostering the arts, and extending the bounds of science'. Though such sentiments were ancient, the new university placed more stress on science, modern literature and economics than did Oxford, Cambridge and Trinity College, Dublin, which were often paraded as models for aspiring colonial universities. However, at the insistence of Barry and the Council (of the eleven councillors, nine had studied at one or other of these three institutions) the classical studies of Greek and Latin, then regarded as the mark of an educated gentleman, were made compulsory in the Arts degree, the only degree offered at this time. They were not compulsory in the matriculation examination established to determine who could enrol for a degree, but their prominence in the degree ensured that they were taught in the private secondary schools that prepared students for university entrance. Cultivated gentlemen were to emerge from the new institution—but not women: they were not admitted to 'the fine stone house in the bush' as the *Argus* described the university.

Its fees, and those charged by the schools, ensured that the university would cater for an extremely small proportion of the population; though, as Victoria had no aristocracy of the British kind, even that proportion had to work for its living. When the university reached its tenth anniversary with an enrolment of only fifty-six students Barry pushed the Council into a crucial decision. Degrees in law and medicine had long been offered at Oxford and Cambridge, but they did not enable their holders to practise their professions; the qualifications required for that were secured outside the university. Barry and the Vice-Chancellor, Anthony Brownless, a prominent medical practitioner, proposed that Melbourne should offer degrees that would contain the academic qualifications required for admission to practise, and thus secure the university a grip over entry to these powerful professions. And, of course, larger enrolments.

Barry, Brownless and the Council, which contained many lawyers and medical practitioners, knew that those professions were troubled by competition from practitioners whose qualifications they regarded, sometimes accurately, as inadequate—though in the days before a 'germ' theory was developed the cures for infectious diseases offered by licensed medical practitioners were often not much more reliable than those used by the competitors they described as 'quacks'. University education gave medical practitioners and lawyers, who faced similar competition, a magisterial and conveniently expensive preparation to mark their superiority over their jostling competitors.

The Medical School building, *c*.1865. The destruction of its elegant portico in 1912 was a victory for unimaginative utilitarianism.

Law appeared as a certificate course for articled clerks in 1858; a Bachelor of Laws was first offered in 1861. Classes for the medical degree began in 1863, shortly before George Halford arrived from England to become the Professor of Anatomy, Physiology and Pathology. He helped to design the medical building erected in the north-eastern corner of the grounds, close to a newly constructed lake that was part of a plan to beautify the university. Meanwhile (in 1861), William Wilson had persuaded the Council to establish certificate courses in surveying and civil engineering. Engineering seemed an appropriate study in a society that was developing the facilities for European-style civilisation—roads, water supply systems, the telegraph, ports, harbours, schools, hospitals, courts, prisons, mental asylums. However, it attracted fewer students than medicine or law: engineers continued to prefer apprenticeship as the means of professional preparation. By 1875

Frederick McCoy, a controversial palaeontologist who did his best scientific work before he left England, but established the National Museum, now Museum Victoria.
(State Library of Victoria)

William Wilson, a revered, choleric mathematician who died while observing the transit of Venus and marking examination papers.
(Trinity College, University of Melbourne)

enrolments, 189, had trebled those of a decade earlier and were more than double the University of Sydney's: law had 60 students, Arts 56, medicine 52, and engineering 27 (a few students had enrolled in more than one course).

The founding professors were active in the city's clubs, churches and societies; they edited periodicals, wrote leaders for the *Argus*, and held senior positions in the Royal Society and in the Public Library of Victoria. Wilson assisted in the negotiations which resulted in an observatory (now the Old Melbourne Observatory) being built in the Domain, and Martin Irving, the replacement Professor of Classics, was a major figure in the establishment of

The National Museum. This is now the site of the Student Union, which on its eastern front retains a small architectural reference to the original building.

amateur rowing. McCoy had a reputation in England and Ireland as an important if controversial palaeontologist. He persuaded the university to establish a botanic garden for teaching purposes in the north-western corner of the grounds and he convinced the government to transfer to the university the museum it was developing in the city. The resultant building became 'the National Museum' and attracted more visitors to the university in the next four decades than did any of its other activities. Based loosely on the design of Oxford's science museum and sited on the opposite side of the lake to the Medical Building, it provided McCoy with the facilities to pursue his palaeontological studies. He was less successful when he declared that the deeper Victorian quartz miners dug, the less gold they were likely to find. The mining industry heaped scorn on his views and continued to find gold at depths where McCoy had said none existed. The university's partnership with industry had made a shaky start.

A Professorial Board, consisting of the professors, the Chancellor and Vice-Chancellor, was established to handle the university's defining task, the education of its students. The Board made recommendations to Council on courses, the setting of texts, teaching, examinations and student discipline, as well as matters that concerned the professors personally, such as their salaries or housing. Disputes immediately arose, especially over compulsory classics, which the Council favoured and the Board opposed. Though the Board had professional expertise, the Council had the power, and the relationship between them grew tense.

The establishment of a Senate in 1867 had increased the tension. The Senate elected new Council members and might reject but not amend the Council's legislation. The Act had stipulated that Senate could not be established until the university had one hundred graduates with masters degrees; it would have been much later on the scene had not the Council bestowed Melbourne masters degrees without examination on holders of masters degrees from approved universities. The professors (except McCoy, who had no degree) qualified for Senate membership. The sometimes acrimonious elections of members of Council and the Senate's consideration of the Council's legislation were reported in the newspapers, especially the *Argus*. The Senate, therefore, was a mechanism for the public discussion of university issues.

Seeking to avoid controversy in a colony riven with political and religious dispute, the university established a public secularity: theology was not to be taught, religious tests could not be applied when admitting students or appointing staff, no professor was to be in holy orders or to lecture on political or religious topics, and lectures outside the university required the Council's permission. An attempt by Hearn to enter parliament greatly annoyed Barry, who feared that the university's political neutrality would be compromised—Council swiftly passed a statute forbidding professors to sit in parliament or belong to a political association. When a faculty of law was

Neither restless political ambition nor autocratic habits diminished the influence of William Hearn's teaching or the range of his scholarship.

George Halford, the powerful and difficult first Dean of Medicine, found that being a grand old man was more satisfying than fulfilling his early promise as a medical researcher.

established in 1873 (a faculty of medicine followed three years later), Hearn secured election as its dean and declared that he was no longer a professor, though he retained his professorial salary and life-long tenure. Dr Hearn, as he was now called, later won a seat in the Legislative Council and success-fully argued that as he was not a professor the statute did not apply to him.

The university's determination to keep out of political and religious controversy was made easier to sustain by the manner in which it defined controversy. Though in the 1860s few issues were as divisive as evolution (*The Origin of Species* was published in 1859), Halford denounced the theory and Darwin's supporter, Thomas Huxley, in mocking public lectures. McCoy provided a stuffed gorilla from the museum to enable Halford to illustrate his case and also wrote a pamphlet whose title, *The Plan and Order of Creation* (1870), made his position obvious. Neither man was disciplined for taking part in the controversy, though their status as leading scientists made their intervention newsworthy and each had religious as well as scientific objections to evolutionary theory.

The Council had stumbled on a policy it was frequently to adopt: views in agreement with those held by the majority of its members were usually regarded as uncontroversial, even if they were the subject of serious criticism in and outside the university; views which challenged those of the majority of Council were likely to be considered controversial. Some topics were too controversial to be discussed at all. When the orthodox Halford proposed to lecture on protoplasm, which raised the possibility of a completely materialistic explanation of life, the Anglican Bishop of Melbourne, Charles Perry, persuaded Council to refuse him permission.

In the light of such attitudes the fate of a student critic is revealing. In 1876 James Hackett wrote to the *Daily Telegraph* under the pseudonym 'Not a Medical Student' criticising the behaviour of medical students at that year's commencement. This ceremony, a source of trouble to the authorities for decades, was held at the start of the academic year and included the conferring of degrees on those who had completed their courses and were thus beginning their life as graduates. The students had jostled each other in the Quadrangle where they had gathered before the ceremony, flung a broom around in a game of pitch and toss, rushed rowdily into the library on the first floor of the North Extension (a recently built addition on the northern side of the Quadrangle's north wing), disrupted the Governor's arrival by singing popular students' songs, and drowned out his efforts to make a speech. Hackett and other critics regarded this behaviour as middle-class larrikinism led by the medical students. 'An Undergraduate', another letter-writer, described these students as 'the rowdiest men in the shop', thus incorporating into Melbourne students' slang 'The Shop', an expression used to refer to Oxford and Cambridge universities. It became the students' casually affectionate name for the University of Melbourne for almost a century.

The students identified 'Not a Medical Student' and brought Hackett before the President of the Professorial Board, Herbert Strong, who had replaced Irving when he resigned to become headmaster of Wesley College.

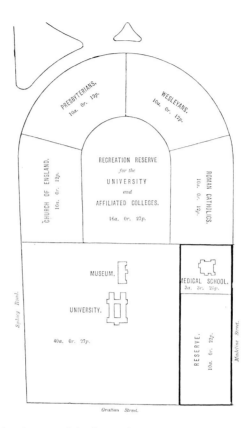

Map 1 The university grounds in about 1870. The land reserved for colleges (none was yet built) is shown, but the lake between the Medical Building and the Museum is omitted (see Map 2 for its position). The Quadrangle (called, as it often was, 'the University') is optimistically shown as complete, but a century was to pass before the south wing was built. (*Melbourne University Calendar, 1878–80*)

Strong suggested that they draw up an apology for Hackett to sign. After a mock trial in the Medical Building he signed an apology, but was nevertheless forced to walk through the lake: as it was less than a metre deep, anyone thrown in might have been seriously injured. Despite some protests against

Wilson Hall: a place for pomp, circumstance and examinations.

'lynch law', Brownless, the Vice-Chancellor and self-proclaimed father of the Medical School, suggested that Hackett be suspended from his studies for a year. Four students who had played a leading part in the trial and the lake incident were given a private reprimand, while Hackett, denied the right to defend himself publicly, was humiliatingly reprimanded by Strong before the assembled student body. A professorial board that rated criticism of medical students as a more serious offence than intellectual and physical bullying had done little to establish a tradition of freedom of speech.

The university's public profile was boosted in 1879 when Barry presided over the laying of the memorial stone of Wilson Hall, the product of a gift of £30 000 from Samuel Wilson, an extremely wealthy pastoralist. The largest benefaction the university received until well into the twentieth century,

Bella Guérin was to describe the Labor
Party, after the First World War, as a
man's harness for women to work in.

the money was used to construct a Gothic Revival building which served the
university on ceremonial occasions and fulfilled Barry's desire for a 'great
hall' to match Sydney's. Wilson Hall was placed close to the east wing of the
Quadrangle. A plan to match it with a similar building close to the Quadrangle's west wing was not implemented, and later generations were left to
wonder why, when so much space was available, Wilson Hall cramped the
original building and towered over it. Its imposing interior witnessed many
ceremonies, though students entered it most frequently for examinations.
Wilson was disappointed in his hope that his gift might secure the hereditary
baronetcy he coveted. He did, however, receive a knighthood.

◊ ◊ ◊

In December 1883, at one of the first graduation ceremonies held in Wilson
Hall, Julia Margaret (Bella) Guérin became the first woman to graduate from
an Australian university. More than a decade earlier two headmasters of girls'

schools had asked that girls be allowed to sit for the matriculation examination. They were not primarily concerned to have their pupils enrol at the university but wished to use the examination as public recognition of the work done in girls' schools. John Bromby, the Headmaster of Melbourne Church of England Grammar School, privately assisted a student, Mary Creed, in her matriculation studies and, when she passed the examination, supported her attempt to sign the matriculation roll, the ceremony that signified admission to the university.

She was refused permission, Bishop Perry having persuaded Council to declare that the Act and the statutes did not authorise the admission of women. He argued that it would divert women from their natural function as wives and mothers, and expose them to physical and mental strain that might damage their bodies and minds. He believed that the natural social order would be threatened if women were given 'unfeminine' appointments such as a bishopric or a high political office. They might also become less marriageable: a weary husband, returning home from his medical or legal labours, would not respond favourably to a wife who wanted to discuss mathematics or legal or medical questions.

John Madden, a rising man who was to become Chief Justice and Chancellor of the University, in neither of which positions he excelled, used the Senate to challenge the Council's decision, though he knew that the Senate had no legal power in the matter. Delaying tactics deadened his attack, but the issue was revived by Charles Pearson, previously a lecturer at the university and headmaster of Presbyterian Ladies' College who, after losing an election he fought in the liberal interest, was rewarded with a commission to review Victorian education. His *Report on the State of Public Education in Victoria* (1878), one of the most lucid and far-sighted ever written on Australian education, helped to renew pressure for the admission of women.

Despite prolonged resistance from the conservatives, Council agreed that from 1880 it would admit women to all corporate privileges of the university except entry to medicine. As men occupied the positions of power in the university and government, the admission of women had to be engineered by them. Bromby was typical of a group of professional men whose support was influenced by their realisation that their income would not enable them to provide sufficient capital for unmarried daughters, who after (and perhaps before) their parents' death would have to earn their own living. The University Act (1881), an emasculated version of a Bill proposed by Pearson, reaffirmed women's right to admission.

◊ ◊ ◊

The women who began attending the university, like the men already there, were required to wear academic gowns on formal occasions such as commencements, at lectures and when in the Library, the Museum and the Quadrangle. This requirement was not removed until the eve of the Second World War, though especially in the 1920s and 1930s adherence to it was often lax. The respect for matters of the mind it was intended to instil found early expression in the Forensic Club, inaugurated in 1860 by a Barry oration during which he announced that, next to the preaching of the Gospel, the law was the most exalted cause in which the human intellect could be enlisted.

The Forensic Club seems to have faded by the 1880s, but that decade saw the establishment of societies to honour Dickens and Shakespeare, the Science Club, the University Musical Association, the Engineering Students' Society, the Articled Clerks' Society (which soon developed into the Law Students' Society) and the powerful Medical Students' Society. The Melbourne University Christian Alliance was also established at this time, the Council overcoming its secularist scruples. Its political scruples were put aside to allow the establishment of a University Militia Corps. And the Melbourne University Masonic Lodge was consecrated at the Masonic Hall in 1891 in the presence of three hundred of the six hundred university masons who had been invited. Neither this association nor the militia, nor the societies connected with the professions of engineering and law, admitted women students.

The sporting clubs were deeply influenced by the belief, adopted from the English Public Schools, that team sport assisted character-formation and empire-building. That one day a team sent from the university might play cricket against Oxford and Cambridge was to many staff and students an

First intervarsity boat race, between Melbourne and Sydney. Melbourne's crew approached the start, according to the *Illustrated Australian News*, 'with a long reaching stroke which spoke volumes for their condition and training'. They won the race. (State Library of Victoria)

inspiring thought: playing the right sort of games against the right sort of people strengthened the bonds of class as well. Cricket was played almost as soon as it could be, in the summer of 1855–56, and a university cricket club established in 1856 or 1857. The Melbourne University Boat Club began in 1859, the year in which the university's football club played its first match, an early version of Australian Rules football in whose development the club played a part. In 1870 the first inter-university sports were held: predictably cricket played at the Melbourne Cricket Ground, and rowing—a boat race on the Yarra. In the 1880s these sports were still being played, though the cricket and football clubs went out of existence from time to time. By then tennis had reached the university, and women students were permitted the use of the university courts, though sexual segregation was practised. Lacrosse, a quin-tessentially middle-class sport, had become popular and the annual university athletic sports were social as well as sporting events. Attempts were made to establish a University Athletic Association to unite all the sporting clubs,

Union officer bearers, 1890. Professor John Elkington is surrounded by confident men looking to conquer the world.

but for the most part they worked separately, combining from time to time when it suited them.

Students and staff had other ambitions that found inspiration in the ancient English universities. The Oxford Union and its Cambridge equivalent provided a model: the famous debates, the prestige of the Union presidency, and the library and clubrooms where members were provided with experiences, acquaintances and social skills that helped their later careers. The Melbourne University Union, a male institution (though women could attend the literary discussions, public lectures, musical evenings and debates) began in 1884 in two rooms of an empty professorial apartment in the west wing of the Quadrangle. From a small office in these often smoke-filled rooms young men produced the *Melbourne University Review*, a magazine that chronicled and analysed the life of the university. It was the second university journal, the first, *Speculum*, having been produced by the Medical Students' Society about two days earlier after an edgy competition for the honour of being the first to publish. A third journal, *Summons*, was started by the Law Students' Society in 1891. Competition between the journals prefigured later battles as the Union, intended to be a meeting place for staff and students, struggled to win support, particularly from medical students.

Required to study in a pervasively male atmosphere, a group of women in 1888 started the Princess Ida Club, which aimed to forge a bond between women, both students and graduates. Gilbert and Sullivan's *Princess Ida*, first performed in Melbourne the previous year, made fun of Tennyson's poem, *The Princess*. As Princess Ida had established a women's university, which like the newly formed club would admit no male members, the significance of the name was obvious. So was some ambiguity: Gilbert had ensured that love triumphed, and by the end of his operetta women had reverted to their accustomed role.

The enthusiastic student life of the 1880s and 1890s was assisted by the establishment of the church-controlled colleges. Situated to the north of the university, across the road that later acquired the name Tin Alley (in honour of the corrugated-iron fence that lined it), the colleges stood on sixty acres (24 hectares) reserved for this purpose when the land was granted to the

Redmond Barry's considerable services to the university deserved a better memorial than the 1960s-cheap building named after him.

Anthony Brownless was a Barry loyalist who shared his conservatism but lacked his charisma. Unlike Barry he needed the chancellorship to reinforce his self-importance.

university by the government. They represented a compromise: the university was secular, the colleges church-controlled; the university received government funding, the colleges none (except the original land grant); the colleges were affiliated with the university in a somewhat obscure relationship that did not give them power over any of the university's activities.

Four colleges had been opened: Trinity, the Church of England college, in 1872, the Presbyterian Ormond College in 1881, the Trinity College Hostel for women students (later Janet Clarke Hall) in 1886, and Queens College, controlled by the Methodists, in 1888. Land reserved for the Catholics, less wealthy than the other denominations and preoccupied with financing their own school system, lay unused until Newman College was built in 1917. Before the establishment of the colleges, students came to the university for their classes and returned to their homes or to nearby boarding houses. By contrast, the colleges provided a group of students for whom participation in clubs, societies, the editing of a magazine, the militia or the Christian Alliance required no travel.

Redmond Barry died in 1880. He had survived an attempt by Irving (elected to Council after resigning to go to Wesley) to persuade the Council to end his chancellorship and appoint William Stawell, the Chief Justice. Not until Raymond Priestley, who came as a full-time vice-chancellor in 1935, did any senior administrator match Barry's contribution. Though obdurately conservative and authoritarian, he could sometimes accept defeat; he kept the councillors' personal ambitions under control, was a persistent advocate of the university's case with government and, unlike some later chancellors, enjoyed the prestige of the chancellorship without regarding it as the main reason for accepting the position. Stawell succeeded him; but when he found that his opinions were not accepted with the awe he thought his judgments were, he resigned. By the time he did, his inability to persuade the quarrelling councillors to his or any shared way of thinking had become embarrassing. His resignation led to a deplorable interlude of almost four chancellorless years throughout which a majority of the Council opposed Brownless's succession because he was uninspiring and a Catholic. As alternative candidates who lacked Brownless's second disqualification shared his first, agreement was hard to reach. In July 1884 James Moorhouse, Perry's successor, was nominated by Hearn and elected Chancellor.

Hearn's presence on Council came as a result of the 1881 Act which, in response to solid professorial lobbying, enabled members of the university staff to stand for election to Council. The number of staff, especially professors, expanded rapidly in the early 1880s because of increased enrolments and the Council's acceptance (after a protracted struggle) of the need to widen the range of subjects offered. Demands were made for the appointment of a professor, a public sign that a field of knowledge was valued, in sciences such as chemistry and biology, which were of fundamental importance in their own right and essential studies in the expanding medical course. In addition a group of schoolmasters on Council were insistent that parents, on whose fees the existence of their schools depended, wanted not only a wider range of sciences (at matriculation and in the university) but also English language and literature and 'modern' languages such as French and German.

In response to such demands the Council appointed five professors in late 1882. The call of the Australian Natives' Association for the appointment of locals was becoming louder. Nevertheless the Council's decision to abandon its London committee, advertise locally and briefly, make the five appointments on the day that applications closed and offer them all to Melbourne candidates was an appalling capitulation to local pressures. Some appointments were made on the basis of letters that were written on the day applications closed and did little more than announce that the letter-writer was an applicant.

Henry Andrew, the Lecturer in Natural Philosophy and a member of Council, had argued for the advertising of the chair to which he was then appointed, that of Natural Philosophy—one of the two responsibilities of William Wilson, who had died in 1874. (Edward Nanson had already been appointed to fill the other responsibility, mathematics.) William Kernot, like Andrew a pupil of Wilson and a lecturer, was appointed Professor of Engineering. John Kirkland followed a similar progression to become Professor of Chemistry, as did Harry Allen, who took some of Halford's responsibilities by becoming Professor of Descriptive and Surgical Anatomy and Pathology. Two of these four (Andrew and Kirkland) were distinctly unsuccessful appointments; the other two, Kernot and Allen, might be considered mixed blessings.

The fifth appointment made on 27 November—Edward Ellis Morris to the chair of Modern Languages and Literature (he had to cover English, French and German in both fields)—was also extraordinary. Not long before the meeting he had resigned as headmaster of Melbourne Grammar School amid some controversy. Through his powerful contacts in the city and the university he knew that the Melbourne professorship was likely to be created, but delays in advertising it and his need for a salary led him to apply for a chair in English at the University of Adelaide. He was appointed in early November, leaked this information to the papers immediately he received it, and did not apply for the Melbourne position but let it be known that he would accept it if it were offered to him. The Council, pressed by one of his closest friends, Alexander Leeper, the Warden of Trinity College, made that offer at the 27 November meeting.

At about this time two other professors were appointed without any advertisement at all. In 1879 John Elkington, a protégé of Hearn who had been appointed Lecturer in History to ease Hearn's load when he became the Dean of Law, was appointed Professor of History. In 1886 Henry Laurie, also a lecturer, was appointed Professor of Philosophy, though one Council member warned that the appointment would be another example of a method of selection they had all abused. Ironically Laurie was to be the one outstanding success among this group of appointments, though Morris also proved valuable. Elkington's was a very troublesome appointment.

Securing the right for professors to sit on Council raised hopes that the relationship between the Council and the Professorial Board might improve. Such hopes faded swiftly, then died entirely after Moorhouse left Melbourne to become Bishop of Manchester. Hearn, who with McCoy and Andrew was a member of Council, was elected as the University's Chancellor in May 1886, the first member of staff to obtain the position. An inspiring teacher (he numbered Henry Bournes Higgins, Alfred Deakin and Isaac Isaacs among admiring ex-pupils), Hearn divided his professorial colleagues. By August he had lost the support of most of them, especially the medical professors, Halford and Allen. Hearn also inherited two disputes which were not of his own making: Allen and Nanson were pursuing salary claims for relatively small amounts to which their entitlement was debatable. Hearn's failure to support them did not assist his cause.

Hearn also opposed a Medical School plan to have the Melbourne Hospital transferred from its site at the corner of Lonsdale and Swanston Streets in the city to a strip of land on the university's eastern boundary, running north from the corner of Grattan and Swanston (then called Madeline at its university end) Streets. Melbourne Teachers' College was later built on part of this land (see map 2). The university had not been granted the land but had obtained some for the original Medical Building and pursued every opportunity to secure the rest. Hearn and the Council argued that land reserved for educational purposes should not be granted to a hospital, even if some teaching took place there. The proposal was defeated, principally because of opposition from forces outside the university. However, the victory was costly for Hearn: he had lost the support of the largest faculty in the university (in 1886 medicine had 214 students, Arts 166, law 61 and engineering 9).

In early August that year Halford took the unprecedented step of calling a meeting of the university's staff on a Saturday. The meeting concluded that it was prejudicial to the university's welfare for any salaried officer to sit on the Council. Of the seven professors present, five supported this decision. The timing of the meeting was not fortuitous. Hearn's five-year term as a councillor was soon to end, and if he were not re-elected to Council he could not be re-elected Chancellor. Sir Archibald Michie, a prominent lawyer and politician, was persuaded to stand against Hearn in the Council election, and a bitter and public campaign to win the support of the graduates who made up the Senate's membership erupted.

Hearn's high-handed action in investing £6000 of the university's money in a bank of which he was a director, instead of in the university's bank, weakened his position. So did unflattering letters to the press from his professorial colleagues. Hearn replied with a manifesto to members of the Senate in which he dissected the character and attainments of these professors with a feline and malicious precision of which none of them was capable. On the day of the election Allen, who had become Dean of Medicine, published a letter explaining why not a single professor, lecturer or examiner in the Medical School would vote for Hearn. Hearn was defeated, narrowly but clearly, and an emotionally exhausted university turned to Brownless as chancellor.

As the Hearn dispute began to develop, Council had in June 1886 approved the building of six professorial houses in the university grounds:

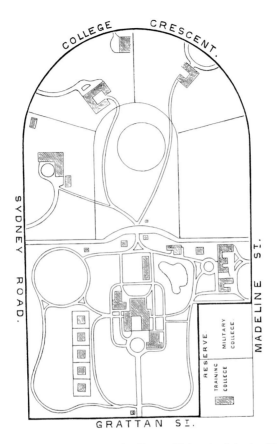

Map 2 The university grounds in 1891(*Melbourne University Calendar, 1891–92*)

one, for the Professor of Medicine, close to the Medical Building, and five on the western side of the grounds. Side by side and about 120 metres from Sydney Road, they would run north from the corner of Grattan Street and Sydney Road. These houses (and one that had earlier been built for Nanson near McCoy's botanic garden) were a long-awaited continuation of the policy that had led to inclusion of professorial apartments in the Quadrangle. In 1887 selected members of a feuding professoriate moved into the double-storeyed, red-brick buildings.

The professors' standing had been seriously damaged, especially as the anti-Hearn professors (the majority) had publicly abandoned the arguments they had deployed when trying to have a clause included in the 1881 Act permitting salaried officers to be elected to Council. Halford, Andrew, Allen and others now declared that professors with seats on the Council had voted on their own salaries, house allowances and similar matters as well as pushing their professional interests. Some professors had (few more zealously than Andrew himself), but the professorial reversal of view exposed them to mockery and reinforced the belief that salaried staff could not be effective councillors.

A professorless Council decided in 1889 that the university needed a paid vice-chancellor, or principal or provost, to use terms then employed. The long-serving Registrar, Edward à Beckett, after a dispute with some professors over examining, offered to resign on an annual pension of £450 so that the Council could appoint a principal 'or some such high and important officer with large and increased powers and corresponding responsibilities and duties'. He contended that the Council had no control over the university's main work, its teaching and examining, and that the Registrar was neither empowered to get the necessary information nor qualified to criticise the work of the lecturers or professors. By May the Council had prepared a draft statute for a provost, an ancient term with ecclesiastical connotations that was still being employed in English, Scottish and Irish universities.

Subject to the Council, the provost, who was described as the university's chief executive officer, was to control the university's office, grounds, buildings, student discipline, commencements and similar ceremonies, conduct the correspondence, arrange the business to be laid before Council, attend Council and prepare all statements of accounts, estimates, receipts and expenditure. The provost was to be an *ex officio* member and President of Professorial Board, have access to all records, inform himself of the work done by professors, lecturers and examiners, and arrange the examinations in consultation with the Board and the faculties. He could require any staff member to explain apparent derelictions of duty. The ghosts of past battles haunted the statute.

The professors opposed the suggestion and disputed the overseas precedents that the Council had invoked. Professors, they insisted, had been appointed as 'the most competent authorities' in their particular areas of study, and no one man could control or supervise the teaching and examining in all the university's departments. The Board offered a counter proposal. Claiming that the swift reorganisation of the Registrar's department was the university's greatest need, it recommended accepting à Beckett's offer to resign because a rearrangement of his duties would be more easily accomplished with a new registrar. It also proposed that the Council should give the President of the Professorial Board most of the powers it was planning to bestow on a provost: safety lay in such a proposal, provided the president continued to be elected by the Board from its own membership. If the statute went ahead, the Board claimed, faith with the staff would be broken, the law strained and the university organised on the model of a school. The provost was the Council's servant, the Board said, so that the proposal turned professors and lecturers into the servants of a servant.

Council approved the statute in August 1889 and sent it to the Senate. After angry negotiations the professorial opposition was successful, largely because the government was reluctant to provide the necessary money for the provost's salary. The proposal lapsed, temporarily, amid the privations into which the 1890s Depression plunged the university.

◊ ◊ ◊

Before the disruption of the Depression, the Council made two important decisions. The first was to allow women to enrol for medicine, a possibility denied them when they were admitted to the University in 1880. Two women, Lilian Alexander and Helen Sexton, led the campaign that secured this concession. Aware that their chances would improve if they could show that other women wished to enrol for medicine, they placed an advertisement in

The first women medical students, 1887: (*left to right, seated*) Clara Stone, Margaret Whyte, Grace Vale, Elizabeth (or Annie) O'Hara; (*standing*) Helen Sexton, Lilian Alexander, Annie (or Elizabeth) O'Hara. According to *Melbourne University Review* in 1887, 'the lady students are, and evidently with the approval of Council, to some extent using their attendance at lectures as a cloak under which they can, unsuspected, carry on their designs to snare the unwary male animal'. Of this group, only Margaret Whyte married.

the *Argus* in January 1887. It drew replies from six women, nearly all from comfortable though not necessarily rich middle-class families. When the Council agreed to discuss their request, Alexander and Sexton, who had sufficient social confidence and contacts to obtain access to important men, interviewed every councillor; on 21 February Council approved their request by ten votes to three.

As the three negative votes had come from medical men, the Council asked the Medical Faculty to comment. It argued that female students should fulfil all the conditions prescribed for admission to degrees in medicine or surgery. This was code for saying that men and women students should attend common (or 'mixed') lectures on all subjects. The Council recognised the code, agreed that men and women students should undergo the same training, but asked the faculty to provide separate lectures for those subjects in which it was 'undesirable on the grounds of decency that the lectures should be attended by both sexes in common'. It also expressed its desire that women should be allowed to enrol for medicine that year. Allen, as Dean of Medicine, swiftly sent Council a letter from the surgeon, Tharp Girdlestone, which identified parts of his surgical course where, he claimed, it was impracticable to lecture to 'a class of students comprising both sexes': 'the venereal diseases, diseases of the bladder & stone, all surgical diseases of the male & female organs of generation, with practical instructions in the use of instruments & appliances required in these affections'. In Girdlestone's view 'ladies' would also require separate instruction in 'the surgical operations on the dead body' and in much clinical work in the hospital wards.

Neither Allen nor the Medical Faculty supported the provision of separate classes, and Allen put two choices to the Council. The first was the complete separation of male and female students as occurred in London, where a separate School of Medicine for women had been established. This, he declared, was radical, expensive and could not be provided in Melbourne in the near future. The second was simpler but unpopular: teaching a mixed class of male and female students. Allen then claimed what he knew to be false: that women students would be prepared to be taught in mixed classes. But, he insisted, such classes would not suit male students nor enhance the Medical School's reputation. In mixed classes embarrassed teachers might avoid 'delicate subjects' and male students might dislike asking certain questions. Carried to its logical conclusion Allen's laborious argument required the exclusion of women from medicine: he offered Council a choice between the financially impossible and the undesirable. However, though willing to march down the road towards exclusion, Allen was careful not to arrive

Harry Allen was one of the first
Melbourne graduates to be appointed to
a chair. His longevity, prominence in the
profession, political toughness and
lengthy occupation of the medical
deanship earned him a knighthood.

publicly at that destination. Instead, he and the Medical Faculty insisted on the mixed classes to which the women students were opposed.

Because the first year of the course involved science subjects only, the debate did not delay the women's entry to medicine, though they worked with the anxiety of wondering what would happen in second year. For month after month the battle between the Medical Faculty and Council continued, the Council insisting on separate lectures, and the faculty remaining adamant that mixed classes were essential and hoping that they might deter women from entering the course or force them to drop out quickly. Fear that this hope might be realised drove Madden to produce the bizarre suggestion that men and women students should be separated by a screen so that they would be saved 'the embarrassment of looking each other in the face'. As the *Age* and some Council members recognised, the Medical Faculty, having failed to persuade the Council to keep women out of medicine, was insisting on mixed lectures in an attempt to frighten them off.

Such lectures have been the norm for so long that it is now difficult to recognise that insistence on them was a misogynistic attempt to set up a hurdle too high for the women to jump. But in the late 1880s such a strategy had some chance of success. For many people, including the women seeking to be doctors, mixed classes raised the spectre of public embarrassment and a confrontation with deep sexual anxieties which the conventions of Victorian society kept precariously at bay. The classes challenged the already threatened ideal of the Victorian middle-class woman as sheltered, refined, pure, a dutiful daughter, tender wife, gentle mother. A society that built separate swimming baths for men and women was threatened when women students in the company of men examined male bodies, treated male sexual diseases and took the scalpel to the bodies of dead men in dissecting classes or to the bodies of live men in operating rooms.

Late in September, as the teaching year moved towards a close, the Council met the Faculty in a desperate attempt to secure a solution. When asked why there could not be separate demonstrations and dissections, Allen claimed that it was unfair to have 'one demonstrator for 200 boys and another for half-a-dozen girls'. Halford's opinion was that 'The female medical students are not girls—they are half-men'. The conference broke up decisionless, and the next day the women students moved decisively. All seven of them wrote to the Council and released their letter to the press. Stressing the 'urgent need of educated women to attend women', they claimed 'the right to qualify ourselves to attend upon the sick and suffering of our own sex'. They agreed that most of their course should be done in common with men, but

> to insist upon attending dissections, hospital practice and certain courses or portions of courses with men would have the effect of rendering the permission you have granted us to study practically worthless, and would be repugnant not only to our own feelings, but to those of the majority of this community.

They would discontinue their course if the 'comparatively few' concessions they required were not granted. After further bargaining the Council secured

Orme Masson, a handsome, impressive
and powerful man, built a distinguished
research school, though his own
research suffered in the process.

agreement from the Medical Faculty that dissecting and hospital instruction would be taught separately, while everything else was taught in mixed classes. For the women students this became a famous victory.

◊ ◊ ◊

Council's second important decision was to reject a proposal to establish an additional chair of classics. The proposal envisaged a professor of Latin and a professor of Greek, as was common in the British universities, and not a single professor of classics—now Thomas Tucker, who had replaced Strong in 1886. Instead, in a symbolically important action, Council advertised for a professor of biology to join the Edinburgh-educated David Orme Masson, who had been appointed the Professor of Chemistry when Kirkland died

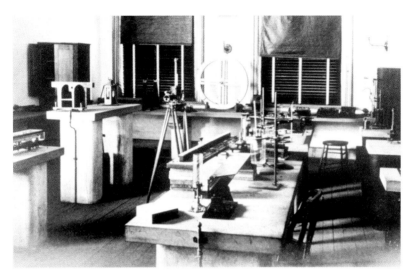

Thomas Lyle's natural philosophy (physics) laboratory, 1892, was a symbol of the university in a changing world.

suddenly. Walter Baldwin Spencer, who had studied at Manchester and Oxford, was chosen for the Biology chair and arrived in 1887; like Masson he preferred to be known by his second given name. When Thomas Lyle, a product of Trinity College, Dublin, was appointed as Professor of Natural Philosophy in 1889 (Andrew had died on board ship while travelling to England), the university secured the third of a triumvirate of science professors who reshaped its teaching and its educational purpose.

Together they advertised the new status of science by persuading the government to provide funds for buildings. They were following the example of medicine, which in 1885 had secured a single-storey building (then called the New Medical Building, now—with a second storey added—Old Pathology), which was sited on the contested strip of land along Madeline Street. Masson enlarged and remodelled the chemistry wing of the original Medical Building, Spencer obtained a biology building on the north side of the lake, and Lyle a natural philosophy building, placed awkwardly close to the north-

Baldwin Spencer and science students and staff, 1894. Spencer and his staff produced a succession of important scientists who were women. Georgina Sweet, seated in the middle, was one of the most significant.

western corner of the Quadrangle to preserve a link with Wilson, who had taught there.

Science's increasingly confident exponents extolled the century's advances. Darwinian evolution with its mechanism of natural selection had introduced a world that did not require a creator, while the geological theories of Charles Lyell presupposed a world immensely older than the Bible's. Dalton's atomic theory, Faraday's demonstration of electromagnetism, and the multiplicity of advances in biology, physics and geophysics, astronomy, meteorology and medicine were changing the intellectual and physical environment in which humans lived. In appointing Masson, Spencer and Lyle the university embraced the promise and power of science and also the technique of which these advances were the product. Thus the systematic use of the findings of observation and experiment, expressed quantitatively and able to be replicated, became for many thinkers the dominant, and for some the only true, model of knowledge.

Masson stressed that the search for 'chemical truth' was of particular importance for a university, more important even than the practical results that flowed from the science of chemistry. The search was a fundamental responsibility for university scientists, and those involved in it— 'researchers'—helped to redefine the university during the twentieth century. For Masson, as for Spencer and Lyle, the university's teachers had not only to disseminate existing knowledge but also to initiate students, or at least a select group of them, into the research culture that created new knowledge.

For one of this powerful trio, research took an unexpected turn. In 1894 Spencer was recruited to an expedition to Central Australia financed by the mining magnate, W. A. Horn. The results of this expedition for biology, zoology, geology and palaeontology were not unimportant, but its fostering of Spencer's anthropological interest was of greater significance. The partnership he developed with Francis Gillen, the postal and telegraph master at Alice Springs, led them into studies of Aboriginal culture that resulted in two major books: *The Native Tribes of Central Australia* (1899)—probably the most important publication to come from the University of Melbourne in the first fifty years of its existence—and *The Northern Tribes of Central Australia* (1904).

Spencer, an evolutionary biologist, was trapped by social Darwinism and viewed Aboriginal culture as the product of a primitive and now dying race. Later in life, as Special Commissioner and Chief Protector of Aborigines in the Northern Territory, he proved to be paternalistic and authoritarian.

But though he and Gillen were sometimes imprisoned in the prejudices of their own culture, they also proved capable of breaking through them. Howard Morphy has claimed that key concepts and themes that later became associated with Aboriginal religion were established by the work of Spencer and Gillen. He lists:

> the network of ancestral tracks that intersect the landscape, the distribution of
> rights in sacred knowledge, the locality-based nature of much ritual practice, the

complex relationship between totemism (or sacred knowledge) and social groups and, perhaps the most significant concept of all, the Dreamtime.

They also helped to pioneer the techniques of modern anthropological field-work and made a considerable contribution to European anthropology, as significant thinkers such as Malinowski, Durkheim and Freud later acknowledged. For a time the University of Melbourne could claim to be at the centre of an international research endeavour.

As the science professors redefined the university's task, belief in the classics as the pre-eminent studies grew weaker. By 1881 only 15 per cent of matriculation students were studying Greek and, though the classics remained compulsory in the Arts degree, they were not compulsory in new degrees such as the Bachelor of Civil Engineering introduced in 1883 or the Bachelor of Science (1888). In Europe the study of philology had gradually placed Latin and Greek under the sway of the laws of linguistics, just as other languages were; so the pretensions of Latin and especially Greek to a superior status were eroded. Their claims to contain the supreme literary exemplars were similarly undermined by the growing view that English, French, German or Italian could cultivate the literary taste more than adequately. The utilitarian claims made by defenders of the classics also came under challenge, especially the reputed usefulness of classical knowledge for the learning of English, or its value as a form of mental discipline. Mental disciplinarians viewed the mind as a collection of faculties that could be trained through exercise (the faculty of memory through learning poetry by heart, for example). This theory enabled defenders of the classics to admit that Latin or Greek learned at school could be swiftly forgotten and yet claim that the experience of learning these languages had been worthwhile because of the mental discipline it had fostered.

◊ ◊ ◊

Discipline had been seriously lacking amid the 1880s building boom. Its collapse in the last years of the decade sent land companies, businesses and banks crashing; with them went the employment of many Victorians who had played no part in creating the boom. Governments applied the received economic wisdom and sought to balance budgets by reducing expenditure. The university's annual endowment, still £9000, could not be cut without a change of the Act, but the supplementary endowment it had negotiated was savagely reduced—from £8250 in 1892 to £3250 in 1896. Over a similar period enrolments fell from 646 to 571, reducing the income from fees from £17 000 to about £16 000. As most of the income from fees was required for salaries, especially for the part-time lecturers who did much of the medical, legal and engineering teaching, the reduction in fee income was more troublesome than it appeared. Salaries were cut, much to the anguish of the professors, who fought harder for their own salaries than they did for those of the lecturers. Economies were made with examination expenses, scholarships, and expenditure on books and equipment, some fees were increased, and the future was mortgaged as maintenance on the buildings and the grounds virtually ceased.

In the early days of the Depression the defence of academic freedom united the professors as, led by Laurie and Edward Jenks, the successor to Hearn (who had died in 1888), they attacked the need to obtain Council's permission to lecture outside the university. Laurie, who had been asked to speak on moral education in state schools, was eventually allowed to deliver his paper, provided he did not raise religious or political issues. The more troublesome Jenks was an outspoken opponent of the proposal for a provost, and lectured outside the university without permission. An irate councillor claimed that it was intolerable that any section of the community should have its opinions, or even its prejudices, flouted by a salaried officer of the university.

Jenks also attacked the administration of the university and the integrity of its Council in the *Centennial Magazine*, a Sydney publication. Visitors to Oxford or Cambridge, he wrote, did not come to see the person who kept the university's accounts or signed the building contracts. They wanted to speak to the historian John Freeman, Charles Dodgson (Lewis Carroll) or Sir Gabriel Stokes, the President of the Royal Society. Melbourne University's reputation in the world of European thought relied on the reputation of its teachers (he named Hearn and Wilson) and not on that of its councillors.

Edward Jenks, first professor of law, was a
bravely outspoken, rigidly righteous,
pioneering constitutional historian.
(Ruth Campbell, *A History of the Melbourne
Law School*)

Further clashes with the university authorities, a rigidity of temperament
which, once a conflict had begun, seemed to make him perpetually intransigent, and personal tragedy—the death of his young wife—led him to resign
and return to England in 1892.

His replacement, William Harrison Moore, made a major contribution to
the Law School, but Jenks's departure was a loss to the university. Apart from
his teaching and his outspokenness, his book, *The Government of Victoria*
(1891), was constructed from sources that no one had previously used and
required an immense amount of lonely work in the Public Library. Few
Victorians, he despairingly noted, would appreciate 'its exactness and impar-
tiality, and the conquest of difficult material', and no one in England would
want to hear about the constitution of Victoria. The book served its purpose
admirably, and is still consulted by some constitutional historians.

Jenks was also a major figure in the establishment in 1891 of the University Extension Board, which provided lectures in city and country areas, given frequently by members of staff on topics of general intellectual interest. The origins of the movement lay in an effort to reform English universities, but neither there nor in Victoria did it to attempt provide access to the university for those who had not been able to obtain entrance in the usual way. It became instead a means of offering classes, which gained no credit towards a degree, to mainly middle-class audiences.

In 1891, shortly before Jenks left, George Marshall-Hall arrived in Melbourne to begin a career which culminated in an even more traumatic confrontation with authority. His chair had been established by a £20 000 donation from the philantrophist Francis Ormond, who was convinced (against the evidence of history) that music improved the moral character of those who listened to it. He considered establishing a conservatorium where students would receive practical instruction as instrumentalists, singers, composers or conductors but, after Melbourne's musical community had debated the issue, he accepted the idea of a chair on the English model. Such chairs were devoted to the scholarly study of music and did not attempt to train practising musicians.

Marshall-Hall fulfilled Ormond's original wish and opened a conservatorium in 1895; as the university was unwilling to do so, he accepted the financial responsibility involved. He was assisted by William Laver, who after studying for seven years in a German conservatorium returned to Melbourne with unrealistic hopes (he was only twenty-two and had not established a brilliant European reputation) of securing the Ormond chair. Later, Laver claimed to have originated the idea of a conservatorium in Melbourne. Marshall-Hall proved to be a brilliant, persuasive teacher who rapidly attracted students, mostly women doing a practical diploma rather than the degree course. He was also an aggressive music critic, a mocker of musical and religious convention, a composer of some importance, and a conductor who made a major contribution to the musical life of the city through the Marshall-Hall Orchestra, which he founded. He published poetry marked more by ardour than artistry.

Like Spencer and Laurie, who supported the Heidelberg School of artists by buying and/or commissioning paintings, Marshall-Hall mixed with Melbourne's artistic community and sat for portraits by Arthur Streeton and Tom Roberts. His professorial status made him valuable to artists who were trying to establish their careers, and his bohemian ways interested students. A whiff of scandal gathered around him when his wife May (née Hunt) returned to England in 1893 with their young daughter. He seems to have become part of a *ménage à trois* with the wife of a Melbourne doctor; after that arrangement ended, apparently peacefully, he formed a relationship with Kate Hoare, by whom he had a son in the mid-1890s. In 1902, after the death of May Marshall-Hall in England, he and Kate Hoare married. He did not live in a professorial house in the university grounds, but his unorthodox behaviour could hardly have remained hidden from his professorial colleagues.

The *Argus* launched a concerted attack on Marshall-Hall in August 1898, and in the resultant controversy two college heads, Leeper and John MacFarland, played leading parts in organising the anti-Marshall-Hall forces; the third, Edward Sugden, defended him. Marshall-Hall had provided a convenient provocation when he used the concert platform to deliver a panegyric on war and Bismarck, who had recently died. 'Life means war, and war is a good thing', he declared; peace on the other hand was for 'invalids and parsons'. His attack on 'the modern petticoat movement' may not have made him many enemies on Council, but mockery of religion did. A popular concert, he announced, was as depressing to a vigorous man as 'a visit to an idiot asylum, or a hospital, or a church'. Three days after this speech, which received wide publicity, the *Argus* attacked his recently published book of poetry, provocatively named *Hymns Ancient and Modern*, after the Anglican hymn book. 'O David was a worthy King', one epigram read:

> *Merrily could he harp and sing.*
> *He became the father of his nation*
> *By dint of prayer and fornication.*
> *He loved his lass, and he loved his Art,*
> *And he was a man after God's own heart.*

The *Argus*, the churches, the religious press, and the leading church and private schools (particularly girls' schools) swiftly united in condemnation, declaring that his love poetry was indecent. He denied the charge.

During the public and intellectually violent controversy Marshall-Hall at first defended himself vigorously, asserting the importance of freedom of speech. Then he was forced to compromise. He argued that his conscientiously held opinions could not harm the university and that, had he been told that the expression of unconventional views on life and religion was not permitted, he would have adopted this view as his rule of conduct. He insisted that he had never said or written anything that justified the claims that he approved of 'indiscriminate sexual intercourse', and he denied that he disapproved of all forms of theism and was contemptuous of those who held such beliefs.

At a crucial Council meeting in October 1898 Alexander Morrison, the headmaster of Scotch College, demanded his dismissal, insisting that he had gone beyond the limits of toleration and that retaining his services was incompatible with the university's neutrality on moral and religious questions. This demand was rejected because there was some legal doubt about whether the Council could dismiss a person for remarks made outside the university. Henry Higgins, usually on the side of tolerance, argued that 'the libidinous character' of his writings and 'his ostentatious parade of disbelief in Christianity' infringed religious neutrality and made many parents reluctant to send their children to the university. Aware that Ormond had insisted that the holder of his chair should be appointed on a five-year contract, and knowing that Marshall-Hall's second five-year term ended on 31 December 1900, Higgins easily persuaded Council to decide that he should not be reappointed after that date.

After this meeting Marshall-Hall became more circumspect in his public utterances, and his supporters felt sufficiently hopeful in June 1900, when debate on his position resumed, to argue for his reappointment. MacFarland, as Chair of the Conservatorium Committee, fulfilled a request from Council to obtain an assurance from Marshall-Hall that his circumspection would continue. In one of the less edifying episodes in the university's history

Anglican Archbishop Field Flowers Goe and
the Argus share a moment in 1898 when it
appeared that George Marshall-Hall might
escape their noose. Two years later, they could
congratulate each other on their triumph.
(*Bulletin*, 5 November 1898, State Library of
Victoria)

MacFarland dictated a statement in which Marshall-Hall declared that he
recognised that policy was the responsibility of the chief administrators of
every institution, that the loyal co-operation of the executive officers was 'the
principle of all order', and that he would 'fall into the policy which com-
mends itself to Council'. Having secured Marshall-Hall's signature to this
statement, MacFarland then took part in the bitter anti-Marshall-Hall

campaign in which the forces that had originally condemned his poetry and anti-religious views again united to oppose his reappointment.

His supporters, including the professors, rallied strongly to his cause, but Marshall-Hall's spirit had been broken. In a statement to the Council meeting on 25 June 1900, at which his fate was to be decided, he unreservedly apologised for his speech at the concert and expressed his abhorrence of some of the meanings placed on his verses which, he said, he would not have published if he had thought they would be interpreted in this way. He even expressed regret for having published them at all. Nevertheless Council reaffirmed its decision not to reappoint him, on the casting vote of its chair, the Vice Chancellor Henry Wrixon, who had put his degree from Trinity College, Dublin, to good use and was now a wealthy and conservative barrister and politician.

Marshall-Hall's only consolation was that he retained possession of the conservatorium, which he had located in Albert Street, East Melbourne: the Council's decision that he should be responsible for its finances had resulted in his signing the lease for this accommodation. Though he set about earning his living by conducting his conservatorium in opposition to the new conservatorium the University was forced to establish, Marshall-Hall applied for the Ormond chair when it was advertised. The Edinburgh-born Oxford graduate Franklin Peterson, an organist and writer of text-books on music, was appointed on the recommendation of a London committee. The Victorian Agent-General, its convenor, seems to have removed Marshall-Hall's name from the list of applicants without informing the committee, though even if protocol had been observed, there was little chance that he would have been chosen. A frightened university had silenced a challenging voice. Hackett, Jenks and Laurie had already found that academic freedom was not deeply ingrained in the university's psyche.

As Marshall-Hall settled in Albert Street and the Depression's austerities continued to erode confidence, the Council was informed in August 1901 that Frederick Dickson, the accountant, had embezzled substantial sums of money. With its fiftieth anniversary looming, the university confronted a calamity.

Power Without Much Glory

The Council had the ultimate responsibility for the university's financial affairs. It determined policy on the advice of its Finance Committee and delegated financial administration to the Registrar, Edward à Beckett, of whose staff Frederick Dickson, the accountant, was a popular member. He had handled the finances with such seeming efficiency that à Beckett's supervision had grown slack, as had the Council's supervision of the Registrar. To complicate matters Dickson had lent à Beckett money, though the Registrar's salary of £800 was £500 a year more than his subordinate's. In an explanation that raised more questions than it answered, à Beckett attributed Dickson's capacity to provide these loans to his winning £1000 on a Caulfield–Melbourne Cup double.

Dickson was arrested and charged with embezzlement on the evening of 28 August 1901, the day on which Council first heard the news. Shock turned into despair as investigations revealed that he had embezzled almost £24 000, more than double what was at first thought and nearly £9000 more than the total government grant for 1900. That £15 000 of the loss had been taken from trust funds holding the donations of benefactors such as Ormond deepened the embarrassment. A Special Committee of four councillors who had not been on the Finance Committee set about putting the university's house in order and negotiating with government. It tightened the administration of the Registrar's Office, reorganised the Finance Committee and the conduct of

Administrative staff, 1894: (*standing*) Edward Bromby (librarian), Frank Gladish (porter), John Steele Robertson (clerk), Peter Marcham (bellringer and porter); (*seated*) J. F. C James (assistant registrar), Edward à Beckett (registrar), Frederick Dickson (accountant).

financial affairs, and recommended that à Beckett should retire from 31 December 1901 with an allowance of £300 per annum. Council lifted the allowance to £350, rejected à Beckett's request for £450 and accepted his disgruntled resignation.

The vigorous John MacFarland, a member of the Special Committee, led the reshaping of the university's financial operations. But the government, preoccupied with cutting expenditure, easily convinced itself that incompetence on the scale the university had managed deserved no easy rescue. Meanwhile the press, especially the *Age*, poured scorn on the Council and the professors, whose Depression-cut salaries had been restored shortly before the defalcations were discovered. On 27 February 1902, the day on which

Dickson was sentenced to five years gaol, a royal commission established by the Premier, Alexander Peacock, began investigating the university's financial position, administration, teaching and government. Chaired by Theodore Fink, a law graduate, landboomer, defender of landboomers and recently the leader of an investigation into technical education, the commission remains the last large-scale, independent investigation of the university's performance.

Its progress report criticised à Beckett's lax supervision, the Finance Committee's uncritical acceptance of Dickson's trustworthiness, and its ignorance of the fact that his operations were virtually unsupervised. It also condemned the Council's failure to define the duties of the Treasurer, a position it had created in 1886 without providing a statute or regulation to guide its operation or to relate its responsibilities to those of the Registrar. The performance of the existing Treasurer, the astronomer Robert Ellery, called for 'the severest censure', the commission decided, finding it hard to understand how the Registrar's incompetence had escaped detection. It was accordingly unimpressed by the Council's decision to lift à Beckett's pension to £350 and by the curious statement that it (the Council) had not insisted on the Registrar's fulfilling his responsibility for the university's financial operation. A wish to be kind to 'an old servant' was the over-generous interpretation the commission placed on the Council's treatment of à Beckett.

The commission placed the main blame on the government auditors: at this time the university had no auditor of its own. Dickson had completely deceived the auditors, and their reports contained embarrassing praise of his skill in keeping the books and his willingness to make them available for examination. The auditors' performance was 'a system where almost every detail is a revelation of either negligence or incapacity'. These finding provided the Council, and particularly Madden, who had become Chancellor when Brownless died in 1897 and had presided over this incompetence for four years, with the opportunity to hide their slackness behind that of the auditors. The commission recommended that the government should make good the money lost through the frauds and that à Beckett's retirement pension should be discontinued.

The government ignored these recommendations and imposed further cuts. After demanding an annual endowment of at least £20 000 and offering concessions, which did not include reducing the Registrar's pension, a humiliated Council was forced into a new round of economies. The lecturers' Depression-affected salaries were cut further, the professors' restored salaries and the value of the university's scholarships and exhibitions were reduced, and fees for matriculation and degrees again increased.

◊ ◊ ◊

The Fink Commission's final report, published in May 1904, announced 'a new ideal': 'the scientific training of the people'. In new countries such as Australia a university should link itself to 'the life's work of the people', especially that which was crucial for economic development. It should offer all branches of literary and scientific knowledge, as well as the practical applications of science, in particular to agriculture, mining, engineering and metallurgy. These studies were to be done at an advanced level, and the 'lower' forms of training left to technical schools such as the schools of mines in Bendigo and Ballarat or the Working Men's College in Melbourne.

The ancient universities of Oxford and Cambridge no longer provided the ideal; instead the commission looked to the United States, Scotland and the new English universities and colleges, especially the University of London. Though knowledge with no immediate practical application

---

Formerly it was doubted whether Universities were the places for Technical Schools of Engineering or Applied Chemistry. This might be debated in England or on the Continent, where there is room for so much specialization, but the question has really answered itself in all new countries, and in a State like Victoria or New South Wales it will be found that the most economic method of organizing the highest education is to include all branches of knowledge, both literary and scientific, and the applications of science within the scope of University teaching, confining lower grades of training to purely technical schools. *The highest Technical School.*

This is the type to which most of the great Universities of America now tend to conform, and which is approached by all the new University Colleges and Universities in Britain, and which is actually recognised by the newly re-organized Scottish Universities, and also the University of London.

The university (Fink) commission's view: the outline of a new but not too strange world. (Royal Commission of the University of Melbourne, *Final Report*, pp. 9-10).

remained important, the commission stressed that the knowledge and skills required for the state's economic, industrial and commercial development (and not simply the development of certain professions) were the university's central responsibilities.

The university's government then came under consideration. Though the Council and senior administration had been exposed as incompetent, the commission first attacked the Senate. It recommended that the Senate should continue to elect councillors but that its approval should no longer be required for statutes and regulations. Wrixon, the Vice-Chancellor, argued for a larger council with unimpeded legislative power and an executive of seven to handle the university's ordinary business and sit in private (Council meetings were open to the press), as did an ordinary board of directors. For all the Senate's rambling debates and other faults, it had acted as a public check on the university administration and as a forum in which graduates could discuss Council's decisions. That power was what the Council, especially its senior members, most resented. They won the commission's support, but their resentment continued as this recommendation was not implemented.

The commission was also worried that the three college heads had been elected to Council, believing that their easy access to the university's authorities made them too formidable. Madden argued that (MacFarland excepted) they should not be on Council, but most professors did not oppose their presence, provided the teaching staff was adequately represented. To newcomers such as Masson, Spencer and Lyle, who had not lived through the trauma of the Hearn affair, the professorial absence from Council seemed extraordinary. The commission eventually decided not to ban the college heads but to ensure that the professors outnumbered them.

Debate on the appointment of a provost did not revive, despite commission support for the policy. Instead the commission condemned the university's 'complicated and retrograde form of government' for excluding the professors, who had the responsibility for teaching. Upon them, it asserted, the task of governing the university primarily lay. It quoted from a letter sent by Professor Ray Lankester, the Director of the British Museum (Natural

History). 'It is an utter mistake for the Governors or Council representing the State to treat "Professors" as servants or "mere employés"', he wrote. They should be 'the real governors and administrators', and the Council should act only on their recommendations and never without their assent. 'The essential idea or conception of a University is that it is a corporation—a Universitas— of teachers, *i.e.*, Professors, who have received from the Crown—the fountain of honour —the privilege of admitting persons who attend their teaching to those honours known as Degrees.' Seeking to affirm Lankester's universitas, the commission rejected the model of university government advanced by Wrixon, and recommended that all professors should be on Council. The proposal was not implemented but its very appearance changed the tone of the debate.

The commission revived the financial proposals made in its first report: the government should take responsibility for money lost through the frauds and for the debit which had derived from the decreases in government grants. It recommended a permanent annual endowment of £24 000, as well as £27 735 for equipping laboratories and £5140 for repairing the badly neglected buildings. The recommendations were accompanied by a comparison with the University of Sydney, whose enrolments had in 1899 exceeded Melbourne's for the first time since the early years. If Melbourne's proposed endowment was added to its income from fees, its annual income would have been almost £40 000—close to the income Sydney received from government grants, fees and two large bequests.

The Fink Commission's recommendations might have amounted to little had not Tommy Bent become Premier in early 1904. In July he produced a Surplus Revenue Bill, which gave the university £10 000 to reduce its liabilities, £2000 for mining and agricultural equipment, and a promise of an additional £12 000 if it could raise a similar amount by public subscription. Greatly heartened, it did so. Bent completed his contribution through the University Act (1904), which provided an annual endowment of £20 000 for the next ten years. Its debts paid, the trust funds replenished and a more generous endowment available for a decade, the university faced a more attractive future.

No.	Candidates' Names.	Greek.	Latin.	Algebra.	Geom. and Trigonomy	English.	History.	French.	German.	Arithmetic.	Geography.	El. Chem.	El. Physics	El. Physlgy	El. Botany.	Result of Examination
133	Moore, Arthur James	—	N	P	P	P	P	P	—	P	P	—	—	—	—	—	Passed
718	Moore, Charlotte Emma	—	N	P	P	P	P	P	—	P	P	—	—	—	—	—	Passed
737	Moore, Walter	—	P	P	P	N	P	N	—	P	N	—	—	—	—	—	Not
251	Morton, Alfred Watson	—	—	—	—	—	Hon	—	—	—	—	—	P	—	—	—	
584	Morton, Florence	—	—	P	P	Hon	—	N	—	P	P	—	—	—	—	N	Passed
934	Mosley, Rupert James	—	P	P	P	N	P	N	—	P	P	—	—	—	—	—	Passed
346	Moulton, Robert Band	—	P	P	P	P	P	—	P	P	—	—	—	—	—	—	Passed
784	Mueller, Ernest	—	P	P	N	N	—	P	P	P	N	—	—	—	—	—	Not
361	Muir, Robert Sibbald	—	N	—	—	—	—	—	—	—	—	—	—	—	—	—	Not
744	Mullins, Bridget Mary	—	—	P	N	P	N	P	—	P	P	—	—	—	—	—	Not
53	Munro, Charles 3	—	N	P	P	—	P	—	P	P	—	—	—	—	—	—	Passed
407	Murdoch, Thomas	N	—	Hon	Hon	—	—	—	—	P	—	—	P	—	—	—	Passed
395	Murdoch, Walter Logie Forbes	Hon	Hon	—	—	—	—	—	—	—	—	—	—	—	—	—	
283	Murphy, Frank J	N	—	—	—	—	—	—	—	—	—	—	—	—	—	—	
429	Murphy, John Joseph	N	Hon	P	P	Hon	P	P	—	N	—	—	P	—	—	—	Passed
36	Musgrove, Frank	—	—	N	P	N	P	—	—	P	N	—	—	—	—	—	Not
975	Sankervis, Arthur Wellesley	—	P	—	—	—	—	—	—	—	—	—	—	—	—	—	
658	Nash, Mary Francis	—	—	P	P	N	N	—	—	P	N	—	—	P	—	—	Not
966	Rattrass, John Hodgson	—	N	N	P	N	—	—	N	—	—	—	P	—	—	Not
258	Neild, Joseph Masters	N	—	—	—	—	—	—	—	—	—	—	—	—	—	—	
112	Nichol, John Robinson	—	—	P	P	Hon	P	—	—	P	P	—	—	P	—	—	Passed
315	Nish, James Alexander David	N	P	P	P	—	—	P	N	—	—	—	—	—	—	—	Not
504	Nixon, Henry Thomas	—	—	N	N	N	N	—	N	N	—	—	N	—	—	Not
524	Noble, Lillian Blanche	—	—	N	N	—	—	N	P	—	—	P	—	—	Not
571	Nolen, Elizabeth Eileen	—	—	N	P	N	N	N	—	N	N	—	—	N	—	—	Not

A page from university's Matriculation Examination Book, 1891. Walter Murdoch, later a lecturer in English at the University of Melbourne and Professor of English at the University of Western Australia, showed promise.

As the head of the state's educational system, in its own and the commission's estimation, the university tackled the matriculation examination. Its standard was so low, the commission said, that students were poorly prepared for university work. Tucker, the classics professor, insisted that the university could achieve much more if the secondary schools provided it with 'better material'. (There seems never to have been a golden age in which the schools supplied the university with the students it thought it deserved.) The commission also concluded that the examination was not an effective test of the 'general culture' of students who did not enter the university.

Both criticisms worried the private secondary schools. In 1903 Victoria had 431 such schools with an enrolment of 24 154. Government secondary schools did not yet exist, but 1988 state schools, with 224 178 students, offered an elementary (primary) education. Virtually all state-school students, like those from Catholic primary schools, went straight from school to work—or unemployment. The private secondary schools had a monopoly on the preparation of students for matriculation.

Aware of the high failure rates at matriculation and the first year of university, the schools pressed for change. Alexander Morrison argued that 'either the standard fixed for it [matriculation] is too low, or the course of study for the first year is too high. In either case, the remedy to be effective must come from the University, which has fixed the standard for both'. Matriculation as a test of 'general culture' was also important to the secondary schools: most students who attempted the examination (and most who passed it) did not enter the university. In 1903, of 1566 students who sat, 478 passed, 367 obtained less than the required number of subjects and only 111 enrolled.

The Council and Professorial Board, anticipating the commission, decided to match the examinations with the students' expectations. They began negotiations with the Senate, the secondary schools, and potential employers of students who did not enter the university. As a result five public examinations were established. The matriculation examination vanished and a more demanding senior public examination determined university entrance. Those who passed could enrol in whatever course they chose, provided they had the prerequisite subjects. A second examination, the junior public, set at the level of the previous matriculation, did not give entrance to the university but marked the end of secondary schooling and tested the acquirement of a 'general education'. Three more examinations were established: the senior and junior commercial and the primary examination, which catered for primary schools outside the state system.

A new administrative structure marked out the path for decades to come. The subjects for each examination were divided into groups—English language and literature, physics, chemistry and so on. The examiners for each group met as a board presided over by a professor, and a Board of Public Examinations, created in 1905 and chaired by the President of Professorial Board, controlled all the examining boards. Its membership included the university, the private and state schools, teachers, and employers. Regulations for all public examinations were to be made by the Professorial Board in consultation with the Board of Public Examinations. Effectively power had been delivered to the Professorial Board, thus satisfying Tucker, who had stressed 'the absolute necessity in a University of having the examinations conducted by the teachers at the University'.

In reorganising its matriculation examination, the university embraced the commission's ideal of scientific training linked to the people's work, an ideal that need not be seen as narrowly utilitarian. Knowledge for its own sake, if confined to knowledge that did not prepare for employment, was more problematic than advocates such as Tucker were willing to admit. 'The "utilitarian" education', he declared, 'satisfies the senses mainly, the intellect inconsiderably, the heart not at all. The liberal culture fills up the measure of the latter two, and rounds off our full humanity.' Many classics students in the Cambridge that had educated Tucker could afford lack of interest in utilitarian studies—in fact wished to display it conspicuously. They came from landed families whose wealth derived from the work of their tenants or employees—an inexact but intriguing parallel with the classical authors who wrote in a civilisation dependent on slavery. Other classics students were headed for clerical livings, schoolmasterships, even bishoprics.

Such arrangements were not possible in Australia, where universities had accepted the responsibility of preparing students for professional life. Properly taught (by Hearn, for example), vocational courses generated an intellectual excitement and a passion for knowledge every bit as profound as the classes that Tucker offered. What mattered most was the teacher's intellectual mastery, passion and independence. Taught without those qualities, even the classics could be reduced to a dreary trudge through texts which were forgotten far more quickly than they had been learned.

◊ ◊ ◊

The university introduced four new degrees that conformed to the commission's ideal, though one, the Bachelor of Mining Engineering, appeared in 1901 before the commission's final report had been issued. It followed the appointment of the English-born John Gregory, a dedicated teacher and vigorous researcher, as Professor of Geology. Students interested in mining had found the geology taught by McCoy, the last surviving foundation professor, scandalously out of date. Only the handful of entrepreneurs who sold notes of professorial lectures to students unable to attend the lectures valued McCoy's laziness: the notes could be reprinted each year without change. His death in 1899 led to Gregory's appointment—and to the transfer of the contents of McCoy's museum to a new building in the city. Baldwin Spencer added the directorship of the museum to his university duties.

Gregory developed geology and mining very effectively but in 1904, depressed at the conditions under which he worked, he resigned to take up a chair in Glasgow. Meanwhile, two professions gained entry to the university for the first time. The handful of formally trained veterinary scientists in Victoria, facing competition from practitioners they regarded as inferior, invoked an English precedent—an 1881 Act that established registration requirements for veterinarians. They secured a Veterinary Surgeons' Act (1887), which established a Veterinary Board to decide the qualifications required for registration and to accredit suitable courses. Rival veterinary colleges battled for recognition, but in 1908 the university set up a faculty of veterinary science and the following year appointed the commanding Scot, John Gilruth, as Professor of Veterinary Science. By 1911 two government-funded veterinary science buildings had been erected in the disused horse market across Sydney Road, within walking distance of the university.

Dentistry followed a similar process. A Dental Act was passed on the same day as the Veterinary Surgeons' Act. A board followed, warring groups of dentists struggled for ascendancy, and in 1904—after Fink's Commission recommended that the Australian College of Dentistry, established in 1898, should affiliate with the university—a faculty of dentistry embodying this affiliation was established. In 1905 the Bachelor of Dental Surgery (later Dental Science) was offered for the first time.

The teaching profession had been debating registration since the 1880s, for the same reasons—self-advancement and the protection of their clients— that influenced dentists and veterinary surgeons. Schools employing inexpert teachers might draw pupils (and therefore fees) from better staffed and more expensive schools. And, of course, incompetent teachers might harm pupils. The Director of (state) Education, Frank Tate, supplied an additional motive by opening the Melbourne Continuation School in 1905. Though he denied that it marked the beginning of state secondary education, the private schools realised that a strong competitor had emerged. That year, while condemning the introduction of government secondary schools as 'state socialism', some of the more powerful private schools supported the passage of the Teachers' and Schools' Registration Act, which enabled the state to enforce standards of building and teacher training that eventually drove many of their smaller competitors out of business.

The university also gained. Tucker, the Dean of Arts, saw registration as a means of halting his faculty's falling enrolments. The academic requirement for registration was the Diploma of Education, the first two years of which were constructed from subjects offered in Arts and science courses; the study of education occurred in the third year. The ensuing increase in Arts enrolments proved Tucker correct, but his staff were not convinced that teachers needed instruction in educational theory or the techniques of teaching, which were also embodied in the diploma. They had themselves learned to teach by teaching, and were well satisfied with the result. The Arts Faculty therefore opposed the establishment of a degree, a chair and a faculty of education. But it accepted the offer of Dr John Smyth, the Principal of the nearby teachers' college, to act as the unpaid Lecturer in Education, it employed Education Department teachers on a part-time basis to supervise the teaching practice, and it watched the enrolments grow.

If education was a dubious blessing, no one doubted agriculture's contribution to the state's economy. During the negotiations that led to the 1904 Act, Bent had agreed, perhaps insisted, that the university should award degrees and diplomas in agriculture. Despite opposition from the Council of Agricultural Education, which conducted agricultural colleges at Dookie and Longerenong, the university established its Faculty of Agriculture in 1906. Students attempting the consequent degree spent three years at the university studying the sciences upon which agriculture depended, and one year in practical studies at an agricultural college. No professorial appointment was made, though Alfred Ewart was appointed the Professor of Botany. Enrolments were disastrous: one in 1906, four in 1907. The introduction of agriculture was an ideological victory for advocates of science-based university training. But farmers preferred learning on the job to attending a university in the city and, unlike in dentistry or veterinary science, no professional group needed university training in agriculture to advance its interest.

Some groups knocked at the university's door without gaining entry. Harrison Moore's advocacy of commerce failed, perhaps because of intellectual snobbishness and the lack of a unified pressure group. And two of the oldest professions, the army and the church, were rejected. Moore led the opposition to compulsory military training, arguing that it was a threat to the university's political neutrality. Leeper's efforts to have theology taught were too obvious an assault on religious neutrality.

While the university moved into new fields, some established faculties struggled. Medicine grew from 249 students in 1904 to 401 in 1914, but was poorly served by its senior staff. Allen had been left in unimpeded authority when Halford was persuaded to retire in 1897 after a drunken intervention at Professorial Board and protests from women students at the jokes he told in lectures. As Halford's teaching had become scandalous and Allen's was never inspiring, the Fink Commission's report of severe criticism from some of the Medical School's staff was hardly surprising. Its research record was not much better. Allen served for four almost research-free decades, which overlapped with Halford's ineffectual thirty-four years.

Heavy failure rates, especially in the late 1880s and 1890s (Allen once failed 64 per cent of his students), an outdated curriculum and unsatisfactory clinical teaching—for most students the key part of the course—increased unrest. Intense competition for positions as honorary physicians or surgeons at the Melbourne Hospital, where the clinical teaching was conducted, grew out of professional ambition rather than eagerness to serve the poor gratuitously: the prestige associated with these appointments often translated into an enlarged private practice. The sometimes scandalously venal elections that decided these appointments did little to reassure medical students or the university at large that clinical instruction would be effective. It often was not, though reforms to the electoral system in 1910 led to a better arrangement.

Many medical students had already left to complete their studies overseas, particularly in Scotland, where they claimed that the teaching, especially the clinical instruction, was better and cheaper. Students who stayed, and some staff, responded that the weaker students left and that Scottish qualifications were easier to obtain. Whatever the truth, medicine was diminished by the exodus. Between 1862 and 1900 it produced almost 500 ordinary graduates. Of the 208 students who left to study at Scottish universities, 154 had enrolled at Melbourne and failed before going to Scotland; all except 5 returned with Scottish qualifications.

Medicine's problems were compounded by its inability to hold good staff. Halford's replacement, the inspiring physiologist Charles Martin, recruited in 1897 from Sydney (he was a product of King's College, London), was appointed as a lecturer because Halford's annual pension was deducted from the money available for his salary. Martin's ingenious and influential research, his determination to pursue it despite meagre facilities, and his laboratory-based teaching lifted the Medical School's standing. For many students he remained a model of what a medical academic should be. Martin resigned in 1903 to become Director of the Jenner (later renamed Lister) Institute of Preventive Medicine in London. He would probably have left Melbourne in any case, but was perturbed by Allen's assumption that a Medical School that had produced him needed little change.

The loss two years later of Thomas Cherry, one of the Medical School's best graduates who had pioneered the study of bacteriology at the university, was a further blow. Annoyed by Allen's determination to supervise his activities, he resigned in 1905 when offered the position of Director of Agriculture. The recruitment of William Osborne to replace Martin and Richard Berry to teach anatomy brought to the university two charismatic teachers who grew to dislike each other intensely. Each did some research, but shortly before the Great War, Alan Newton, a young (and soon to be famous) surgeon, com-

Charles Martin was an inspiring teacher. 'I have lots of chaps always working about the labs and we are very crowded. We are all very happy together', Martin wrote, accurately, to a friend. (*Alma Mater*, vol. 3, no. 3, 1898)

plained that with few exceptions the research done in medicine had been insignificant.

William Kernot, though generous to the university and popular with students, allowed his business interests to distract him. Engineering was severely criticised by the Fink Commission, and Kernot's reputation did not improve when he demanded that a member of staff, Bernhard Smith, should retract the evidence he had given to the commission. Smith refused and eventually lost his lecturing appointment. Many government departments, councils and other employers still refused to accept engineering graduates unless they sat additional examinations; and Melbourne's degree had not secured that valued token of respectability, recognition by London's Institution of Engineers. Kernot's sudden death in 1909 led to the appointment of Henry Payne, who restructured the school, widened its offerings, appointed new staff and gradually gained recognition for its degrees. He also secured extensions to the original Engineering Building, which had been opened in 1901 in the southeastern corner of the grounds.

The restructuring of the Conservatorium had been relatively swift. Franklin Peterson, though less charismatic, was more politically astute than his predecessor, and enrolments grew respectably, despite competition from Marshall-Hall's conservatorium. Assisted by the patronage of Nellie Melba, the first section of a Conservatorium Building was opened on Sydney Road in 1910; an attached concert hall named in Melba's honour came two years later.

The Arts Faculty's enrolments grew from 123 in 1903 to 405 in 1914, aided by expansion of the state secondary system and the efforts of private-school teachers to meet the requirements of the Registration Act. By 1914 twenty-four high schools and nineteen higher elementary schools had been opened, where a decade earlier there had been none. Though the Registration Act did not apply to government schools, Tate, mindful of comparisons with private schools, sought to staff his new secondary schools well. Furthermore some primary-school teachers enrolled, seeking qualifications for promotion or a transfer to a high school.

The growth in enrolments was assisted by free places for the Diploma of Education, which had been granted to the Education Department during the dark post-Dickson negotiations over the 1904 Act; in any one year they could account for 40 students. In addition, evening lectures had been offered since 1905. Tucker's plan to stress their inferior status by insisting that they have a separate staff from day lectures had misfired: they attracted young and ambitious teachers such as Walter Murdoch and Jessie Webb. Tucker's disdain for the vast majority of his students grew as rapidly as the enrolments. Only honours students were worthwhile, he asserted; now a multitude of pass students (especially state-school teachers, he lugubriously noted) was tumbling into his faculty and, he considered, lowering the standard of the degree.

The university had made a serious, though by no means radical, attempt to assist students from less wealthy families. It had always offered scholarships at the matriculation (now senior public) examination, but on a scale that ensured that they would do what scholarships are usually designed to do: mask privilege rather than assist the poor. All students who passed the senior public examination and could pay their fees, however borderline their performance, were granted entrance to the university; students whose parents could not afford the fees needed to perform brilliantly and win a scholarship before they could enrol. Even if such students won all sixteen of the scholarships available in 1914 (721 students attempted the examination), the university would have absorbed them with no disturbance to its middle-class ways. In fact most scholarships were won by pupils from private secondary schools whose fees excluded all but the financially comfortable. Though they annoyed Tucker, the free places granted to aspiring teachers, and the evening lectures that enabled the enrolment of students who were working for their living, were more effective ways of opening the university to students from less privileged families.

◊ ◊ ◊

Women found teaching a convenient means of entering the university, whereas law was uninviting. Flos Greig (LL.B., 1903), was the first woman to graduate in law from an Australian university and the first to enter the legal profession. The professional barriers raised against the employment of women were such that the Women's Disabilities Removal Bill had to be passed before she could practise. Even so, the legal profession was not flooded with women graduates: the next appeared in 1905 and the third in 1909.

Medicine was easier of access: it was less adversarial than the law, perhaps, and not so overtly linked with power. Nevertheless major difficulties remained. Without seeking to persuade Council to change its ruling on mixed instruction, Allen, usually a stickler for the formalities, twice endeavoured to break the agreement; each time he was defeated. Berry's openness and his lack of historical baggage helped to end the arrangement peaceably, and from about 1910 women attended mixed classes. They had other battles, especially when they began to appear at the top of the class lists and win prized residencies at the Melbourne Hospital. For a time the Medical Students' Society, despite its inclusive name, excluded women students. They established their own society until the older society removed the barrier.

Sport remained significant, though the Athletic Association had collapsed. In 1904 John Lang, ardent amateur and secretary of the Boat Club,

Women students, *c.*1910, outside the eastern
entrance to the cloisters in the Quadrangle's
north wing.

suggested establishing a sports union to develop co-operation between the
clubs. With Spencer's assistance it was established, and Council approved an
annual compulsory sports levy. Assuming that sport was men's business, it
levied male students only, but after protest extended the levy to women. The
example of Oxford and Cambridge remained attractive and in 1905 the
Sports Union first borrowed the concept of a 'blue' as a recognition of selection for inter-university sport, then ploughed through old records to confer
blues retrospectively—even posthumously in some cases.

Of more significance was its decision to establish a magazine to chronicle and comment on the life of the university. *Alma Mater*, an ambitious successor to the *Melbourne University Review* and to the short-lived publications which followed the *Review's* collapse in 1890, had itself closed in 1902. Until the first issue of the Sports Union's *Melbourne University Magazine* (*MUM*) in 1907, there had been no student journal devoted to covering the university as a whole. In the same year, and also growing from the Sports Union, the Students' Representative Council (SRC) was established. Financed from members' subscriptions, it took over *MUM* and, though by no means radical, represented the students' first concerted attempt to participate in the government of the university. Revealingly, one of the Council's first reactions was an unsuccessful attempt to co-opt the SRC's support to improve student behaviour at commencements. In 1910 Spencer persuaded Council to allow the old museum to be used as a student club-house, and thus secured a base for the Sports Union and the SRC.

When the 1904 Act was passed, the university had 615 students; a decade later it had 1375. Though a source of pride, the doubling of enrolments caused financial stress, of which the university was particularly conscious as the ten-year agreement for the government endowment drew to a close. In 1913 the Council established a committee of enquiry into most aspects of the university's life. Academic plans were prepared and ambitious building programmes developed—they included the construction of a south front for the still-open Quadrangle. The government of the university, including the constitution of the Council and the Senate and the appointment of a provost (issues allowed to lapse in the rush after the 1904 Act), was vigorously discussed. Then in 1914 England declared war on Germany, Australia promised its last man and its last shilling, and the university's life, like the country's, was changed.

◊ ◊ ◊

The third Marquis of Salisbury, speaking in 1876 to Britain's Prime Minister, Disraeli, about a proposal to establish an Indian peerage, expressed doubt about the power of the Indian aristocracy. He thought, nevertheless, that if the British obtained their good will and co-operation it would 'serve to hide to the eyes of our own people & perhaps of the growing literary class in India the nakedness of the sword upon which we really rely'. The Australian literary class, so far as it was represented by the university's staff, had no such view of empire, though Aborigines had confronted the sword's nakedness. When war broke out, only two professors, Allen and Cherry (who after disputes in the Department of Agriculture had returned to the university in 1911 with the Professorship of Agriculture to console him), were Australian-born; the others came from England, Ireland or Scotland. All rallied to the imperial cause. Male students, overwhelmingly the product of schools in which the Empire was fervently honoured, enlisted, perhaps not as swiftly as zealots such as Leeper required, but quickly enough to ensure that when the war ended 1723 Melbourne University men had served, 271 of whom were killed.

The war found Marshall-Hall in despair. In 1913, without telling the Albert Street Conservatorium that he did not intend to return, he had gone with his wife and son to England in an attempt to win appreciation for his music on a larger stage. The venture was a disaster and his last hope, a performance of his opera *Stella*, failed, leaving him professionally and financially desperate. Then Franklin Peterson died. Marshall-Hall's Melbourne friends, including James Barrett, now a major figure on Council, launched a campaign to have him offered the Ormond chair. Despite the efforts of Laver supporters such as Leeper and MacFarland, he was offered and accepted the post. He was still re-establishing himself when he died suddenly in July 1915 after an operation for appendicitis. Laver replaced him.

By this time the casualty lists from Gallipoli were bringing home the war's horror. When conscription became an issue Harrison Moore secured from Madden, the Chancellor, an indication that professors might openly support it, though unlike some university staff Moore refused to use his lecture-theatre as a recruiting office. He was aware that such public advocacy in a university supposed to be politically neutral raised awkward questions, but belief in the moral strength of the British cause had engulfed the staff. Some enlisted; others including Tucker, Osborne and Ernest Scott, who was

Mary Clementina De Garis at war.
Formidable, brave and brilliant, she
volunteered for war service after her
fiancé was killed.

appointed Professor of History after Elkington's overdue retirement, delivered patriotic lectures; Berry ran the 5th Australian General Hospital in the Police Barracks in St Kilda Road; and Masson, Osborne and Thomas Laby, who on Lyle's retirement had been appointed Professor of Natural Philosophy, devised an ingenious gas mask.

As the realisation grew that victory was dependent on industrial strength, Masson seized a moment of extravagant enthusiasm from the Prime Minister, W. M. Hughes, to press for a council of science and industry. The campaign had its vicissitudes, but Masson served on the first council of the Council for Scientific and Industrial Research (CSIR—later CSIRO), having associated

Eduard Scharf, internee, c.1914–15
(National Archives, New South Wales)

the university with the establishment of a major research organisation. Masson's protégé, the chemist A. C. D. (David) Rivett, went to England to ease the shortage of skilled professionals in its munitions industry. John Latham, later Chief Justice of the High Court, became Victorian Secretary of the Universal Service League, a pro-conscription lobby group, and enlisted in 1917 as Head of Naval Intelligence.

University women moved into various professional positions to replace men who had enlisted, helped to organise and to raise money for the Red Cross and various patriotic funds, and took part on both sides of the conscription debates. Women medical graduates were not permitted to enlist, but a handful of Melbourne graduates assisted the voluntary medical services provided by British women. They included Helen Sexton, a leading figure in the agitation which led to the admission of women to the Medical Faculty; she helped to start a field hospital in Auteuil and later worked in a Parisian hospital. Mary De Garis became the Chief Medical Officer at the Scottish Women's Hospital in Macedonia, a tent hospital attached to the Serbian Army. Meanwhile Allen wrote poetry of a fervid imperial kind and John Wilson, chair of the Finance Committee and once headmaster of Presbyterian Ladies' College, declared that anti-conscriptionists were 'usually fat, florid, goggle-eyed, broken teeth dishevelled men and women'. Each of Cherry, Barrett, Higgins and Fink had a son killed in action.

Hatred of things German led Walter von Dechend, the Lecturer in German, and Eduard Scharf, a piano teacher at the Conservatorium, to the realisation that the liberty for which Australia was said to be fighting did not apply to them. Born in Germany, both had lived in Australia for many years and married Australians. Neither was naturalised and, despite the efforts of Leeper, who led the public attack and fed rumours to the Intelligence Corps anonymously, neither was shown to be disloyal. Each lost his university position, Masson being the only councillor consistently to defend them. Scharf was interned in 1918, released in May 1919 and eventually reunited with his wife and son, who had been visiting Germany when war broke out and had been unable to return to Australia. In the mid-1920s von Dechend applied unsuccessfully for another university appointment.

Disputes over academic freedom had occurred shortly before the war when Masson decided that material in *Speculum* and *Melbourne University Magazine* was indecent and insulting to women. Some women insisted that they did not need or want Masson to defend them, but negotiations between the SRC and the Professorial Board led to responsibility for a magazine being vested in an editor elected by students and approved by the Board. It reserved the right to move against indecency but stated that it would not interfere with criticism of university affairs. 'So long as you are dull and prudent', an *MUM* poet remarked, 'You'll make the P.B.'s ideal student'.

The eclectic socialist and law student, Guido Baracchi, was neither dull nor prudent, and raised the issue of free speech when he argued in *MUM* in 1917 that the war, 'whatever the jingos and junkers may tell us', was

The war memorial, made less conspicuous when the
south wing of the Quadrangle was erected, never
captured the university's imagination.

essentially a European affair being fought to maintain the balance of power
in Europe. Council asked the Board to consider the disciplinary consequences of his article. Despite the efforts of Spencer, a dedicated imperialist
but a liberal in matters of free speech, Baracchi was accused by Osborne of
disloyalty and charged with misconduct for having published material which
might derail student support for the war. Nanson and Laby sought his permanent expulsion, but the Board severely censured him, stating it would have
imposed a harsher punishment if the censor, to whom Baracchi had sent the
article, had not passed it.

Almost immediately Baracchi published a letter which showed the Board little reverence. He was forced to apologise for the 'offensive terms' in which he had referred to staff and required to make a public statement of his loyalty to the British Empire. He did so. A few days later about two hundred students interrupted a paper he was giving at the Historical Society, rushed him to the lake and forced him to stand in the water up to his boot-tops. The Board conducted no investigation, though the incident was reported in the newspapers. A university crowded with defenders of Empire and freedom had connived at the silencing of challenge.

The university produced its formal war records slowly, as if not wishing to confront the changed world that grew from the conscription debates, industrial battles, losses in the French trenches, shell-shocked minds, and bereavements set to stretch over decades. The *Record of Active Service of Teachers, Graduates, Undergraduates, Officers and Servants in the European War, 1914–1918* appeared in 1926, the year in which a war memorial was placed south of the Quadrangle's east wing. It conferred degrees without requiring further work on some soldiers who had almost completed their studies before enlisting, created six war bursaries to assist the education of students whose fathers had been killed, and agreed not to appoint to a salaried office any person who had been eligible for war service unless he had enlisted or provided an acceptable reason for not doing so. With other universities it negotiated an arrangement through which the Repatriation Department paid half fees for all returned soldiers; it agreed to waive the other half for students needing financial assistance.

◊ ◊ ◊

The returned soldiers brought dramatic change. Enrolments rose from 1204 in 1917 to 2449 in 1922. Shortages quickly developed in teaching staff, equipment, accommodation, laboratories, books and even space to eat lunch. In 1922 Arts/education had 689 students, against the 405 of 1914. Medicine, the most expensive faculty, had 731 students (401 in 1914), and science 230 (58 in 1914). Yet agriculture had only 28 and veterinary science with 19 was slipping

The intervarsity women's hockey team, 1930. They played on a field in the south-eastern corner of the grounds, between the professorial houses and Sydney Road (see map 3), which is now occupied by medical buildings.

Arts/Education (now Old Arts), 1925. Originally Arts (mainly) and education, and with an important administrative section, it has recently returned to the Arts Faculty's sole use.

towards an enrolment of 2 in 1927 and closure. Other developments pulled the university in new directions. An architectural atelier, modelled on the Royal Academy Ateliers in London and the Schools of Beaux Arts in France and the United States, opened in 1919 in a small building near the main entrance in Grattan Street. It grew out of Rodney Alsop's determination that architecture, still located in the Engineering Faculty and taught predominantly as a science, should also be regarded as a creative art. Its members had keys, so that if inspiration struck they could work there at night.

The returned soldiers also brought an edge to student affairs as they set about rebuilding their lives, professional careers and, in some cases, the society to which they had returned. In 1925 a student newspaper, *Farrago*, published weekly during term time, and the Labour Club, were founded. The club's founders overlapped with those of *Farrago*, and included the historian Brian Fitzpatrick, Lloyd Ross, a tutor in history and in the 1930s a Communist union leader, and Ralph Gibson, son of the Professor of Philosophy, William Boyce Gibson, and later a member of the Communist Party. Council unhappily approved the formation of the Labour Club and a rival Liberal Club, which had Ian Maxwell, then completing a law degree, as its president. Guido Baracchi and Esmonde Higgins, then members of the Communist Party, became patrons of the Labour Club. The Public Questions Society, started amidst controversy in 1918 to foster debate on social and economic issues, began to seem anodyne by comparison.

Academic life remained relatively conservative. In the mid-1920s the library moved to the Quadrangle's North Wing from the first floor of the North Extension, where for fifty years it grew steadily and scandalously overcrowded. The new accommodation was immediately revealed as inadequate and, especially in the 'swot vac' before the final examinations, students queued outside waiting their turn to pursue their studies. They were still required to wear gowns at lectures and in the library and the Quadrangle, but did so less enthusiastically. Lecturing was the basic means of instruction and, though tutorials appeared in some courses, they were used as a means of coping with large classes rather than as a vital teaching device. The Princess Ida Club had voluntarily closed in 1915 and women seeking to defend their interests worked through the SRC which, except to those seeking to gain office in it, was not a particularly vital force in student life. The political clubs and the Student Christian Movement, a descendant of the Christian Alliance of the 1880s, were more powerful. The sporting clubs continued, the strongest being those closely connected to sports favoured by the private schools: rowing, cricket, football, athletics, hockey and tennis, in the last two of which women were particularly prominent.

Research foundered in the dislocation of the early post-war years, especially as the small but useful government grants instituted in 1908 had vanished entirely in 1918. They had, however, assisted the work of Henry Grayson, an autodidact who won international recognition on a scale that few of his professorial colleagues achieved by designing a machine for ruling diffraction gratings; it was thus of great value in the measurement of the wave-lengths of light and other spectroscopic work. During the war and throughout the 1920s Berry's research into mental deficiency and brain size was supported by government and the press, its profoundly conservative social, educational and racial implications gaining approval in a country (and indeed a university) where the White Australia policy was an orthodoxy. His public standing may explain his success in obtaining government funding to erect a very large red-brick anatomy building in 1923. The major building of the time, however, was the long overdue Arts/Education (now Old Arts) Building, erected between 1919 and 1921. It featured a clock tower, a reference to the tower included in White's original plan for the Quadrangle's unbuilt south wing.

The crucial unfinished task, the negotiation of a new endowment and organisational structure for the university, involved familiar issues: the membership and functions of Council, the status of the Senate and Professorial Board, the relationship of the staff to Council, and the functions, if any, of a provost—now usually referred to as a salaried vice-chancellor. The formation in 1921 of the Association of University Teachers grew out of dissatisfaction with Council and government, and the realisation by many staff that their interests and those of the still powerful professors did not always coincide. Rivett, now an associate professor and the heir-apparent to Masson's chair, joined the association—'but apparently only to fight them step by step', Masson's daughter, Marnie, noted. His motives were more confused, and for decades his dilemma—wanting to be paid a reasonable salary while hoping that his desire did not look too obvious—haunted many staff in the association.

A University Bill was introduced in 1919, postponed, reconsidered, amended, and reintroduced without being passed. Ad hoc increases were made to the endowment and fees were raised before the University Act was passed in 1923. It provided an endowment of £45 000 with an additional £8500 to set up a faculty of commerce, conduct scientific research, and establish a University Extension Department in place of the ailing Extension Board. The endowment was dependent on the university providing teaching and research in 'science as applied to household management' (a Barrett favourite), admitting fifteen students per year to the Diploma of Education free of fees, providing another fifty free places per year for degrees or diplomas, and admitting certificated state-school teachers and teachers' college students on half fees. The controversial provision for a salaried vice-chancellor lapsed.

The Act established a Council with thirty-one members. Eight were nominated by the Governor-in-Council, and ten elected by Convocation, which had replaced the Senate. The other councillors were three professors elected by the professors, the President of the Board (*ex-officio*), one member of the teaching staff elected by staff other than professors, two elected by the undergraduates, the Director of Education, the Chair of the Council of Agricultural Education, not more than two heads of colleges (co-opted) and two other co-opted members. The Council had been transformed.

The graduate and the general public were the greatest losers. Convocation, a body consisting of all graduates, elected a standing committee, consisting of the Warden and forty members, to exercise the legislative power previously held by the Senate. Where the Senate had elected all members of Council (except three parliamentarians added by the 1904 University Act), Convocation could elect only ten of the thirty-one councillors. Moreover, if its standing committee twice refused to approve a statute or regulation, or amended it in ways with which the Council did not agree, a majority of the whole Council at a specially called meeting could approve the legislation. Convocation had been opened to all graduates, and most power, except that of being a nuisance, had been removed from it. Gone were the Senate's long, disorderly debates in which issues discreetly discussed in Council were publicised and the community given some insight into the university's ways.

◊ ◊ ◊

The decade following the 1923 Act was disillusioning. To many it seemed that an authoritarian and exclusive group had taken control of the university. It included James Barrett, whose intelligence, imperturbable assumption of superiority, and determination to have his way made him formidable. So did his friendship with John MacFarland, who had become Chancellor after Madden's death in 1918.

MacFarland's competence was undoubted. After leaving Ormond in 1915, he pursued a successful business career, holding directorships in the National Mutual Life Association and the Trustees Executors & Agency Co. Unengaged by public intellectual life, he adroitly served the Presbyterian Church (his primary loyalty), played golf, fished and became very wealthy. As Chancellor he seemed to regard bold planning, exploration, even persuasion as risky activities in which the outcome could not confidently be predicted. He offered efficiency and quick meetings, but imaginative administration was beyond him. So was respect for intellectual freedom, as he showed in the Marshall-Hall affair, the dispute over German staff during the war, and in the controversies involving *Speculum* and *MUM* where his sympathies were always with the censors.

When James Darling, Headmaster of Geelong Grammar School, joined the Council in 1933 he found a pattern unchanged since the early 1920s. Barrett sat at one end of the Council table and MacFarland at the other, two powerful men and good friends, with the group they controlled sitting between them. '"Those for? Those against? Carried". This was the nature of Sir John's chairmanship and woe betide anyone who disagreed.' When disagreement arose, Barrett's mastery of detail, including the history of controversial issues (a history which he had often helped to shape) and MacFarland's chairmanship were complemented by the attitude of the Chair of the Finance Committee, John Wilson, a famous pennypincher.

While MacFarland was overseas in 1919 Barrett had established a Details and Buildings Committee which, despite its name, handled important matters. Chaired by Barrett and made up of senior 'outside' councillors and the outnumbered President of Professorial Board, it was a device to ensure that the 'right' decisions had been made before the full Council discussed

John MacFarland in the robes of the Chancellor, a position he held from 1918 until his death, aged eighty-four, in 1935.

Alfred Ewart was an effective and controversial botanist whose intense lobbying kept the Botany Building at the forefront of the Council's mind.

the issues. The committee continued throughout the 1920s and 1930s and, though two professors were added and its powers gradually reduced, it contributed to the outlook expressed in a letter to Rivett: 'the whole atmosphere of the University is bad—there is a complete lack of faith in the ruling clique re scholarship'. And not only scholarship.

The retirement of experienced professors added to the clique's power. The trio of scientists who had reformed science teaching and contributed immensely to the general life of the university had gone by the mid-1920s: Lyle (1913), Spencer (1919) and Masson (1924). Tucker had retired in 1919, and the Council declared Allen's position vacant in 1926 after he had been incapacitated by a long illness. Their replacements proved mixed blessings.

Peter MacCallum, Allen's replacement, was immediately effective and became still more significant in the 1940s; Laby, who replaced Lyle, mixed brilliant scholarship with self-centred and destructive recalcitrance; Wilfrid Agar, Spencer's replacement, proved a fine scholar and an honest administrator, but Rivett, from whom most was expected, stayed less than three years before moving to the Council for Scientific and Industrial Research.

Some powerful figures remained. Ernest Scott, inspiring teacher and reshaper of the teaching of history, was trusted by staff—he was elected President of Professorial Board with instructions to 'watch Barrett'. The respected Harrison Moore, the acknowledged authority on the Australian Constitution, fought the clique vigorously before retiring rather suddenly in 1927. In the same year the more circumspect Robert Wallace, Professor of English since 1911, achieved the higher office he was seeking: he was appointed to the vice-chancellorship of the University of Sydney.

With financial confidence restored by the Act, the university ventured into new fields. In 1924 John Greenwood was appointed the first Professor of Metallurgy. A moribund Engineering Faculty benefited as Greenwood set about changing the teaching to reflect a society that was beginning to manufacture its own requirements as well as being a primary producer of metals and minerals. In the same year the New Zealand-born Douglas Copland became the foundation Professor of Commerce. Ambitious, aggressive and charismatic, he built up the school rapidly. In its first year, 1925, 323 students enrolled; most were part-time, but no course in the university's history had begun with such a flourish. The Commerce Faculty was further advanced by the appointment of the unorthodox Lyndhurst Giblin to the Ritchie Chair of Economic Research in 1928. Samuel Wadham, who became Professor of Agriculture in 1925, admitted that he might have difficulties in working a plough but won the respect of country communities and his university colleagues. That rarity, an Australian-born professor, Thomas Cherry (junior), the son of the university's first Professor of Agriculture, gave decades of distinguished service after he was appointed Professor of Mathematics in 1929. He followed the Shepparton-born violinist and conductor, Bernard Heinze, who was appointed to the Ormond chair in 1925 when Laver resigned after an unexciting term. Creative, ambitious and manipulative, Heinze did not win the respect of all his musical colleagues, but his prominence at the Australian Broadcasting Commission made him a vital power in Australian music. And his children's concerts introduced generations of young Victorians to classical music.

Meanwhile, new buildings appeared. In 1928 Ernest Skeats, the Professor of Geology, moved into a Geology Building immediately west of Berry's Anatomy Building, and the following year the Professor of Botany, Alfred Ewart, opened the elegant Botany Building on the south-eastern corner of McCoy's dilapidated Botanic Garden, now called the System Garden. In 1925 an Agriculture Building had been erected in the north-western corner of the grounds. Other parts of the university struggled. Veterinary science closed in 1927, its main building passing to the Council for Scientific and Industrial Research. The Professor of Veterinary Science, Harold Woodruff, who had been appointed when Gilruth left to become Administrator of the Northern Territory in 1912, was made Director of Bacteriology in 1929, and in 1935 Professor of Bacteriology. He fought hard for the Public Health Laboratory, which had developed out of a bacteriological laboratory established by Thomas Cherry senior.

Education also had difficulties, partly because of its uneasy relationship with the Arts Faculty. After unpleasant negotiations, Smyth managed to obtain a chair in 1918. As the Education Department paid two-thirds of his salary, many members of the Arts Faculty opposed his proposal to establish a faculty of education, believing that freedom of speech might be incompatible with the loyalty Smyth owed to the Education Department. As the same argument presumably applied to Smyth's role as a teacher in the Diploma of Education, but was overlooked in that case, the faculty's position was more compromised than it admitted. Smyth secured the establishment of a faculty in 1923, died in 1927 and his replacement, Leslie Wrigley, a conscientious and cautious man, had done little to unravel the faculty's position and to brighten its teaching when he died in 1933. His replacement, George Stephenson Browne, though not an intellectual heavyweight, was to prove more effective.

Dentistry also struggled. After much negotiation Frank Wilkinson, a medical and dental graduate of the University of Liverpool, was appointed the university's first Professor of Dental Science. His term was made difficult

Noel Counihan studies class enemies. The young left-wing painter was earning a living providing sketches for the society magazine *Table Talk*. The newly arrived Vice-Chancellor, Raymond Priestley, was the central figure. (*Table Talk*, 7 March 1935; Mathieson Library, Monash University)

by disputes with the Australian Dental College and the Dental Board. He resigned in 1933 to go to Manchester and was succeeded the following year by Arthur Amies, a more effective and ruthless academic politician.

Medicine made an important gain under Berry's strong deanship. The desire for a better site for the Melbourne Hospital had impinged on the university during Hearn's brief chancellorship and later. After labyrinthine negotiations between the Council, the Dental and Medical Faculties, the Melbourne Hospital, the government, the Education Department and the Charities Board, an agreement was made in 1926 that the Melbourne Hospital would gradually be transferred to a site in the disused pig market across Sydney Road, directly opposite the University. The Veterinary Faculty's buildings were adjacent to this site. In addition, land was reserved for a new medical school building in the south-west of the university's grounds at the corner of Sydney Road and Grattan Street, behind the row of professorial houses. The Medical School's old buildings in the north-east corner were to be renovated and passed down to other faculties.

Many of the arrangements established by this agreement were not implemented. For a time the area that Berry had reserved for the Medical Faculty was used as a women's hockey field, while the Melbourne Hospital's move to the pig market site took almost two decades to achieve. But Berry had established a site for a medical building in the university grounds opposite the Melbourne Hospital, upon which a later Dean of Medicine was able to capitalise. Barrett's unscrupulous behaviour at this time, especially an attempt to supplant Berry in discussions with the Rockefeller Foundation, greatly angered Berry. Suspecting that Barrett was manoeuvring to end his employment, he resigned at the end of 1929 and took an appointment in England. His replacement, Frederic Wood Jones, an English anatomist of somewhat eccentric distinction, was to command student loyalty in the way Martin had done.

As the Depression of the 1890s had done, the Depression of the late 1920s and 1930s crippled the university. Cuts in government expenditure resulting from the Premier's Plan of 1931 were no more palatable because Copland and Giblin, now major advisors to government, had played a part in devising the Plan. The endowment was reduced by 20 per cent, all salaries over £250

Ethel McLennan established a strong reputation as a teacher and researcher in botany, but was to be passed over for the chair in controversial circumstances.

Proletariat was a journal established by the Labour Club, whose sympathies were bravely obvious. (Education Resource Centre Library)

were to be cut by 15 per cent per annum and those under £250 by 10 per cent. Negotiations led to a cut of 10 per cent across the board, but other cuts—on staffing, laboratories, equipment and the perpetually neglected library—followed. The early 1930s were tense and sour.

One of those years, 1933, was of particular significance for women. It marked the fiftieth anniversary of Bella Guérin's graduation, and the securing of land for the much desired non-denominational women's college—outside the university grounds admittedly, but opposite Ormond College on a convenient block that had once been the Carlton Cricket Ground. The 915 women students of 1933 accounted for 27 per cent of the enrolment (3333), about the norm at this time. Arts had 400, music 171, science 110, education 41 and medicine, in a total enrolment of 535 (Arts had 999) may have had

50 women. Engineering had none, architecture one or two at the most; agriculture and commerce a few. Law continued to be unattractive: between 1913 and 1930 only 10 women obtained the degree of Bachelor of Laws. Teaching was the profession which attracted most university women. Though not a way to affluence, it was respectable and less expensive than law or medicine, especially if an Education Department scholarship came to hand. For some it was an honoured profession gladly embraced; for others it offered the prospect of earning a sufficient income to live independently. Bella Guérin, especially when she was Bella Halloran and a widow bringing up a young son, used it in this way.

Teaching positions at the university remained difficult for women to secure. In 1933 all twenty-four professors were male. Women held one (Ethel McLennan) of the nine associate professorships, three (Jessie Webb, Edith Derham and Ruth Buchanan) of the twenty-eight senior lectureships, and two (Isobel Cookson and Janet Raff) of the fifteen lectureships. On the bottom ledges of the hierarchy, the percentage of women rose: there were six among the twelve tutors and nine among the twenty-two demonstrators and senior demonstrators. In 1933 almost all the full-time women teachers beyond the level of tutor had not married. Georgina Sweet, who was also the first woman in an Australian university to be appointed an associate professor, became the first women member of Council in 1936. From 1853 until then, university government at the highest level, the Council and Professorial Board, was conducted in the absence of women.

From 1932 to 1935 the Labour Club published a journal, *Proletariat*, whose name placed it in the midst of the struggles between fascism and communism, particularly the Russian version, that were convulsing Europe. These tensions were violently expressed at the university in April 1932 during a Historical Society meeting at which Ernest Scott lectured on the 'great Whig historian, Macaulay', a symbolic choice of topic. A nineteen-year-old Jewish Ukrainian appreciated the symbolism. Samuel Weinchelbaum (Sam White)

THEIR TURN to sing the
National Anthem.—Two stu-
dents, after having been thrown
into the lake, had to sing God
Save the King before their cap-
tors would allow them to go.

Sam White and colleague in the lake. Intellectual bullying was left unchallenged by
Council and Professorial Board.
(*Sun News Pictorial*, 4 May 1932; State Library of Victoria)

began a lengthy explanation of Marx's interpretation of history, and Scott
eventually remarked that the meeting was not prepared to listen to 'buffoons
or baboons' and criticised White for his behaviour, not his opinions. Four
days later White spoke at the University Debating Society in the Public
Lecture Theatre. Edward 'Weary' Dunlop, recalled that he was furious that 'a
very small minority of Communist sympathisers' could generate 'a tremen-
dous publicity about the red university'. On an agreed signal he and a group
of sympathisers seized White, forced him out of the lecture-theatre and were
heading for the lake when a squad of police arrived. White was not thrown
into the lake and returned to finish his speech. The next day a *Farrago* editorial recounted Baracchi's 1917 adventures, reminding its readers that out-
raged undergraduates had forced him to 'apologise or *embrace the lake*'. That
afternoon three students including White were forced to walk through a lane
of students from the Union Building to the lake. The front page of the *Sun*

A yabbying contest, 1935, was a more peaceful use for the lake.

carried pictures the next day of one of them lying in the mud beside the lake, and of White and another student standing in the lake singing the National Anthem, as they were required to do before they were released.

The silence of the Council and Professorial Board was compelling. Their minutes contain no reference to the debate, the editorial or the 'embracing' of the lake that had been forced on White and his friends. The Board seems to have passed the matter to the SRC, safe in the knowledge that from this SRC no disciplinary action was likely to follow. None did.

John Monash's death in October 1931 precipitated a crisis. He had been elected Vice-Chancellor in 1923, partly to ensure that Barrett did not obtain the position. As conditions deteriorated under the retrenchment measures, resentment towards the 'junta', as Wadham called it, increased. MacFarland,

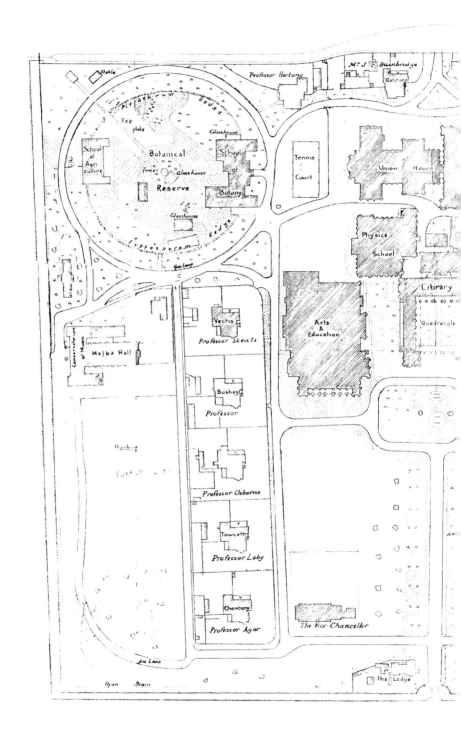

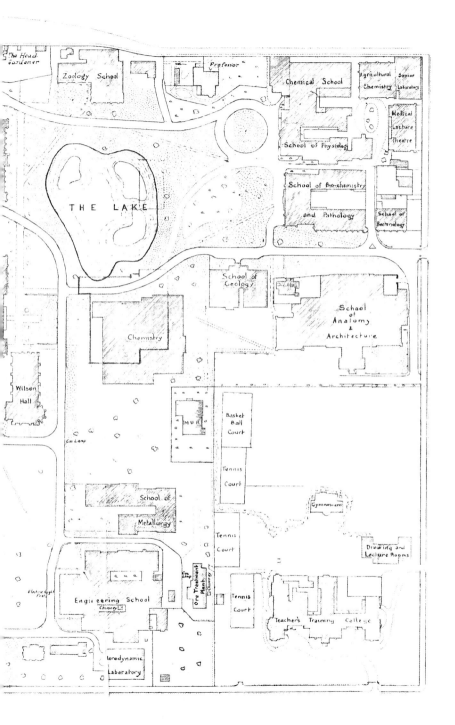

Barrett, and Wilson had long angered staff, and their cautious reaction to the cuts increased dissatisfaction. F. W. Eggleston, an acute observer, believed the university's leaders went to government, pointed out that they had balanced the budget, were thanked, and departed. The possibility that Barrett might now replace Monash as vice-chancellor, and be well placed to succeed MacFarland if he resigned or died, alarmed many staff.

On Sunday 11 October 1931, in a mourning coach returning from Monash's funeral, some senior professors including Kenneth Bailey, Harrison Moore's replacement, decided that the time had come to establish a paid vice-chancellorship. The longlasting fear of the power that such a person would hold had collapsed before the greater fear of Barrett's interventions. Their first task was to revive the issue, for after extensive debate the Council had agreed to the appointment of a paid vice-chancellor in August 1928 and set up a committee to discuss the position's salary, qualifications and duties. Neither MacFarland nor Barrett was keen, other controversies emerged, and when Monash died nothing had been done. Though those in the mourning coach and their allies acted immediately, Robert Menzies did not steer the required Bill through parliament until 1933. The search for a suitable appointment in Australia and overseas revealed that Rivett had overwhelming support. In 1934 he was offered the position and declined, partly because, or so he told Barrett, he would not have enough money left after the necessary entertaining had been done.

The Council then turned to a strongly recommended Englishman, Raymond Edward Priestley, a Cambridge graduate (B.A., 1920, Dip. Ag., 1922), who was assistant registrar, secretary to the board of research studies and secretary-general of the faculties at Cambridge. He accepted the position. Earlier in the year, at the Oxford and Cambridge cricket match, Darling had walked up and down behind the pavilion at Lord's trying to persuade Priestley to come to Melbourne. If his arguments were influential, Darling had reason to be pleased: Priestley was to prove a dynamic, if a somewhat enigmatic, vice-chancellor.

Previous facing pages: Map 3 The university grounds in about 1935: a campus growing crowded. (Property and Buildings)

A Place No Longer Apart

Early in 1935 Raymond Priestley arrived in Melbourne to take up the duties of the university's first full-time vice-chancellor. He had come from Cambridge and his familiarity with Australian universities dated back a quarter of a century, to a brief period at Sydney when he assisted its professor of geology to write up their findings from an Antarctic expedition. Priestley remained at Melbourne for less than four years. He was succeeded in 1938 by another Englishman, John Medley, an Oxford graduate and briefly a Cambridge fellow, who by this time was running an Anglican school in rural New South Wales.

Priestley was offered the Melbourne post after a distinguished Australian scientist, David Rivett, rejected it. Medley won the vice-chancellorship in an acrimonious contest with Douglas Copland, the Dean of Commerce. Neither of Melbourne's first two academic leaders claimed scholarly eminence and neither could draw on any significant experience of academic duties, at least in a teaching capacity. They brought instead the urbane assurance of educated Englishmen serving in the Dominions and the cachet of association with ancient seats of learning—the absence of prior involvement with the local academic community possibly enhanced their appeal to the local business and professional elite that controlled the university. Even so, Medley's principal backer, an industrialist, had to warn him it would be impolitic to stay in the Melbourne Club while he pursued his candidature.

The new Union House, built from
donations, opened in 1937. Priestley wanted
a facility for students, staff and graduates to
meet and share in university life.

Raymond Priestley took office as Vice-
Chancellor in 1935, determined to 'temper
professional training with the liberal spirit'.
Frustrated in his endeavours, he appears
here on the eve of his return to England in
1938.

Both men surprised the oligarchy that appointed them. Priestley was
astonished on his arrival to find an institution that was so threadbare in its
facilities, so poorly housed and understaffed. He also realised that the

impoverished character of the university betrayed its low standing in the community and the stultifying conservatism of its Council. His forthright efforts to put the university on a new footing brought him into conflict with several of the oligarchs and led to his early resignation. Medley saw many of the same defects—an interfering Council, quarrelsome professors, a parsimonious government and unappreciative public—but moved more skilfully to overcome them.

When Priestley described the University of Melbourne as 'financially starved', he acknowledged the high standards many of its 'outstanding personalities' maintained in their teaching and research. In arguing for improved amenities and conditions, his overriding goal was to enrich the experience of students. Of all the building projects that he cajoled from the Council, the state government and private benefactors—the yellow-brick Chemistry Building, the Commerce Building with its greystone bank façade, Percy Grainger's idiosyncratic museum—there were two that symbolised his understanding of a university. At the centre of the campus, the Union House would provide a meeting-place for students, staff and graduates. On the southern edge, the Vice-Chancellor's Residence would enable him to participate fully in university life. Priestley's aim was to create an academic community.

Medley, who shared the same ideal, formed a shrewd appreciation of the local circumstances that operated against it. The Australian university, he wrote in retirement, struggled with poverty and isolation. The result was a narrow homogeneity, for there was not enough money for 'bold experiment', and with just one university in every capital city there was not enough competition to stimulate variation. 'The average Australian matriculates at $17\frac{1}{2}$, goes into a professional school at his university, and qualifies for entry to the earning arena as soon as possible.' Hence the common view of the university as a '"shop"—a place to get out of quickly'. The redeeming element, thought Medley, was the students. Each university attracted 'the best brains of its State', since there were few counter-attractions, and these gifted undergraduates sustained an 'intense extra-curricular activity' in political, cultural and social pursuits.

In 1935, when Priestley arrived at Melbourne, there were 3500 students and nearly 1000 of them were part-timers. The Commerce Faculty, with 457 enrolments, was made up almost entirely of evening students from the city. Agriculture (63), architecture (37) and dentistry (82) were faculties in miniature; there were a couple of hundred in education, engineering, law and music; 332 in science, 651 in medicine and 933 in Arts. The 915 female students were concentrated in Arts, music and science. While the university was open to any student who matriculated from secondary school and its enrolments were on the rise, less than one in fifty Victorians in the 17–22 age group gained admission. The fees, which ranged from £22 to £37 for a year's tuition (the minimum weekly wage for an adult male was just over £4), formed one barrier; living costs presented another. The several hundred free places and scholarships had little significance for pupils in most government schools, which did not teach to the university's entrance level.

Three-quarters of the male undergraduates therefore came from the private schools, and clustered in the university's residential colleges. These colleges were a particular feature of Melbourne University, imposing in their architecture and dauntingly effective in transmission of social values. They offered lodging, devotions, additional tuition and pastoral care, sport and companionship that emphasised the gulf between their residents and the majority of students who commuted daily from home to campus. There were four denominational men's colleges and just one for women residents, though a new, non-denominational Women's College opened in 1937.

To teach the 3500 students there were 25 professors, some 75 other full-time academic staff and as many more part-time assistants. The two professors in the Faculty of Law were its only full members of staff. Bernard Heinze, the Professor of Music, kept up a remarkable level of performance as the conductor of the university's Melbourne Symphony Orchestra, but his faculty's tuition as well as its conduct of the Australian Music Examinations Board relied on a small army of part-time teachers. The largest of the thirty or so departments (Physics and Chemistry) ran to 10 and 7 full-time members respectively, while half a dozen small departments had but one established position.

Teaching under such circumstances relied heavily on the rote lecture and the textbook as devices to transmit a corpus of received knowledge, and the examination to ensure it was absorbed. There was a thriving market in lecture notes, past exam papers and model answers. Laboratory and tutorial classes were restricted to the upper levels of study, encouragement of intellectual inquiry to the abler students who made up the honours lists. The library was utterly inadequate, with a collection of just 90 000 volumes, so that those writing essays in more discursive subjects depended on the Public Library. The professional faculties prescribed a set curriculum and bonded their students in a common experience; students in Arts and science, who ranged more freely, were likelier to enter into university life.

Customs and rituals enclosed students in a world that was poised between childhood and adulthood. When you entered the university you acquired the title of 'Mr' or 'Miss'. The males wore collars, ties and hats; the suitcoat or blazer was only now yielding to the sportsjacket. Gloves, hats and stockings were still obligatory for females. Yet before the cafeteria opened in the new Union House, most students brought their own cut-lunches. Apart from those enveloped in the boarding-school regime of the colleges, few undergraduates lived locally. The daily routine of most—a morning journey by public transport, then classes, before the afternoon journey back to the family home—hardly differed from school.

The undergraduate body was highly conscious of its status, however, both on the campus and beyond it. The university's annual commencement ceremony early in the first term was an occasion of high-spirited irreverence. As part of the same carnival, students processed in the retail sector of the city, ostensibly to collect funds for charity, in practice to cause maximum disruption with stunts and flour-bombs. Later in the year, the University Revue lampooned respectability in song and verse; it was staged in a city theatre even after the Union House offered a local venue.

Scatological humour was one aspect of undergraduate life, earnest civic engagement another. Sensitive to the privileged position they enjoyed in a place of intellectual inquiry, some students assumed both a right and a duty to prick the public conscience. With the growing international threat of

During the annual commencement celebrations, students processed through the city and conducted stunts. Suitably attired, the engineering students of 1935 are ready to go.

The University Revue, staged each year in the city, was an occasion of student exuberance. In this publicity shot, the dance group rehearses. (*Farrago*, 8 April 1946)

fascism and war, these activists were drawn to the progressive politics of the popular front. The Labour Club, the Student Christian Movement and the Peace Society now exerted a powerful influence on the Students' Representative Council and *Farrago*, the student newspaper.

The university had never lacked critics. Indignant correspondents of the metropolitan newspapers would regularly censure the excesses associated with student japes. Those members of the university who challenged political orthodoxy, however, incurred far more vehement condemnation in press and parliament: their actions were thought to damage the standing of the university and imperil its public support.

The Australian university was particularly vulnerable to such fears. It was a civic university, established by government to serve the public interest, supported with public money and expected to conform to community standards. Control was vested by now in a governing body largely composed of graduates prominent in the professions and public life, who kept a close watch on the conduct of both staff and students. The intention was to protect the university from adverse publicity in order to safeguard the annual grant; the effect was to seclude it from the life of the community, which in turn felt little need to contribute to its welfare. An appeal for the Union House went out to 7000 graduates; in the first year of the campaign just 177 of them responded with donations.

The Council of the University of Melbourne was distinguished by its frugality. Melbourne lagged well behind Sydney both in the size of its government grant and the value of its endowments; equivalent civic universities in England operated with several times its income. Herbert Brookes, a leading Melbourne businessman, was said to be 'awestruck and appalled at the university's poverty and the rigour and parsimony of its financial procedures' when he joined the Council in 1933. Newcomers to the university, for that matter, were struck by the dilapidation of the fabric: the experience of sitting in draughty, unheated lecture-theatres during the winter term recurs in the memoirs of students of this period.

Melbourne's Council was also jealous of its powers, habitually considering every detail of administration (and since the only administrative officers were a registrar, an accountant and two chief clerks with a support staff of little more than a score, it had ample opportunity to do so). The decision to appoint a vice-chancellor as the chief executive officer of the university came some time after Adelaide and Sydney had taken that step, and acknowledged the manifest deficiencies of leadership, but even then the Council oligarchs were reluctant to surrender control. Priestley's difficulties came to a head in 1937 after a rowdy debate in the Public Lecture Theatre over the Spanish Civil War.

James Barrett, who by now was Chancellor, backed by John Latham, his Deputy and also the Chief Justice of the High Court, demanded that the Vice-Chancellor provide a report of the meeting. Priestley refused, and the Council eventually conceded that the Chancellor had no executive functions. Several of the professors urged Priestley to demand the resignation of Barrett, but he did not and soon after resigned himself. Medley, his successor, was put up by a section of the Council against one of the more outspoken professors, and accordingly faced significant reservations among the staff. He moved quickly to win their confidence, consulted widely and worked closely with the key academic forum, the Professorial Board. Priestley's fortuitous appointment of a new Registrar, John Foster, strengthened Medley's administrative control. In 1939 he moved decisively to dethrone Barrett. Latham, who succeeded him as Chancellor, accepted the new regime.

Much of Priestley's time as vice-chancellor had been spent planning and proselytising. He had secured support from the Carnegie Corporation to tour North American universities and also for a conference of Australian and New Zealand universities, held in Adelaide in 1937 (at which a national union of students was also formed). Medley, who inherited his predecessor's survey of the university and its needs, was more pragmatic. 'The business of a university', he once stated, 'is to temper professional training with the liberal spirit'. On another occasion he put it more bluntly: 'we educate in vast mobs, and yet produce narrow specialists'. His 1939 memorandum on 'University Needs' set out the need for more appointments ('teachers enough to dissipate our mobs') and further buildings, which could only be financed by drawing on reserves. The outbreak of war quickly vindicated the decision.

An equable, sympathetic man, Medley worked best with the professors, whose foibles he recorded in verse:

> *Professor Laby*
> *Is behaving like a baby.*
> *He would not get so cross if he*
> *Cultivated a little natural philosophy.*

In a hierarchical institution where most of these men ran their departments with absolute authority, decision-making at the university level was inseparable from the personalities of those who made them. Medley had great respect for Samuel Wadham, the formidable Professor of Agriculture, for Kenneth Bailey, Professor of Law, and for his younger colleague, George Paton. He quickly recognised the acerbic brilliance of Frederic Wood Jones, the Professor of Anatomy, whose resignation in 1937 was a serious loss. Wilfred Agar (zoology), Thomas Cherry (mathematics) and irascible Thomas Laby (physics) were eminent in their fields. In the Medical Faculty an older generation was passing and Peter MacCallum (pathology) was joined by Sydney Sunderland (anatomy) and R. D. (Pansy) Wright (physiology), while in Arts A. R. Chisholm (French), Max Crawford (history) and Boyce Gibson (philosophy) confirmed the growing trend for Australian appointments.

◊ ◊ ◊

Medley appreciated that the professoriate, which he emancipated from the tutelage of the Council, itself constituted another oligarchy. He was less concerned than his predecessor to promote broader participation; Priestley had encouraged the Students' Representative Council to share responsibility for campus life. Some of the non-professorial staff felt Medley took little interest in their aspirations. The female staff had particular grievances. In his final

Georgina Sweet became the
university's first female associate-
professor in 1920 and the first female
Council member in 1936. For
seventeen years she led the
provisional council that established
Women's College.

Thomas Howell Laby, a miller's son from
Creswick, was Professor of Natural
Philosophy (1915–42) and a Fellow of the
Royal Society. An irascible controversialist,
he stormed out of meetings that did not
agree with him.

months Priestley had disappointed those who hoped that Ethel McLennan
would be appointed to the chair of botany. She was an associate-professor in
the department, with a significant research record, but a younger man from
Cambridge was preferred. Melbourne's first and only other female associate-
professor was Georgina Sweet, a retired zoologist, who had opened the
appeal for the Women's College with a donation of £1000. As an elected
member of the Council, she asked it to overturn the recommendation of the

selection committee. After lengthy debate the appointment of the man was confirmed. Five women in the Department of Botany wrote to express their disappointment. One of them, Margaret Blackwood, would become the university's first female Deputy Chancellor—more than forty years later. John Turner, who won the chair, would name the Botany field station on Phillip Island after Ethel McLennan.

Women received little encouragement to pursue academic careers. The patterns of preferment favoured men, who were more likely to study abroad after their first degree and far more likely to catch the eye of a selection committee. An able young man displayed promise, his female counterpart was expected to choose between marriage and vocation. The career prospects of female graduates were similarly handicapped: a ban on married women in the public service forced many who wanted to teach into the private schools, while less formal restrictions impeded advancement in other professions. The University Appointments Board, which assisted graduates find employment, took little interest in 'those who had husbands to support them'. Females were active in the clubs and societies, yet few held office. The indomitable 'Ding' Dyason, who entered the university as a science student in 1938, was able to compare the 'noisome infamy' of the three ladies' toilets in the old student club-house with the vastly improved provision in the new Union House; she was convinced that toilet facilities provided a quantitative index of sexism.

Other changes to the fabric of the university indicated its makeshift renovation. The Union was located to the north of the Quadrangle, chemistry and commerce to the east, the Grainger Museum on the western perimeter close to Melba Hall, the Vice-Chancellor's Residence by the Grattan Street entrance in the south. Yellow brick was the most common medium, contrasting with the earlier stone and more recent red brick.

A pattern was hard to discern: medicine and engineering had been dispatched to eastern extremities of the campus; agriculture and botany were on either side of the System Garden to the west; other activities moved out of the Quadrangle as new accommodation permitted. Large palms lined the drive from the main gates in Grattan Street to the Quadrangle, and a row of

An aerial view in 1938 shows the Chemistry and Commerce buildings under construction; the lake has disappeared, along with most of the Moreton Bay fig trees outside Wilson Hall. The Grattan Street entrance and the row of professorial houses are visible at the top.

professorial houses was off to the side. But the chief feature of the sylvan campus, the University Lake, was filled in with the construction of the Chemistry and the Commerce Buildings. Since it had served in the past to punish dissidents with a drenching, the loss of amenity brought an enhancement of freedom.

Priestley's energetic lobbying for support brought a further change. He persuaded the City Council to take over responsibility for the grounds in return for opening them to the public. Hence by 1939 the campus lighting went from gas to electricity, and the lamp-lighter no longer made his way around the university each morning and evening. Most of the Moreton Bay fig trees outside Wilson Hall came down, and so too did most of the iron railings that marked off the university as a place apart.

◊ ◊ ◊

When Melbourne's vice-chancellor called for a more expansive role for his charge and greater support for its activities, he proposed that 'the boundaries of the State should be the boundaries of the University'. Some time later, the leader of the country with the most extensive university system warned of the dangers of too close an identification. The proper role of the university, the President of the United States declared, was to serve as 'the fountainhead of free ideas and scientific discovery'. He feared that the infusion of vast quantities of public funding into universities raised the prospect that the demands of the State might dominate the nation's scholars, so that 'a government contract becomes virtually a substitute for intellectual curiosity'.

Between Priestley's confident aspiration and Dwight Eisenhower's mordant warning a global conflict conscripted all the intellectual resources of the combatants. If the Battle of Waterloo had been won on the playing fields of Eton, then the outcome of the Second World War was decided on the laboratory benches and production lines of the Allies. After the awesome power of science was demonstrated on the cities of Hiroshima and Nagasaki, there was a further contest for supremacy among the victorious powers that demanded of the academy an even greater service of the national interest. Both the World War and the subsequent Cold War enhanced the significance of the Australian university. It became vital to the country's scientific and technological capacity, essential for augmented levels of specialist expertise, an indispensable source of advice on issues of policy and administration. As the boundaries of the university expanded to meet the growing demands of the state, its capacity to nurture free ideas came under strain.

The limits of dissent were tested at Melbourne as early as May 1940, when the 'phony war' ended and German forces invaded France and the Low Countries. Thirty-one of the staff, including half a dozen professors, wrote to the newspapers in protest against the Australian government's censorship of communist and trade union publications (the Communist Party had opposed the war and in the following month would be declared illegal). The Professorial Board was so alarmed that it arranged for staff to disassociate themselves from the letter; most did so, though twenty-five held out. James Barrett, no longer Chancellor but still an interferring councillor, demanded that all staff take an oath of loyalty. Medley resisted him and the Council backed the Vice-Chancellor, who expressed his own feelings in *The Scarlet Letter, May 1940*:

> *So there aren't any Communists*
> *In Melbourne University.*
> *They've been hunted from their hotbeds*
> *Of Unmentionable Vice.*
> *And the world now smiles*
> *On the Melbourne University*
> *Converted to a Frigidaire*
> *Of Obscurantist Mice.*

The original thirty-one miscreants had written again to the press to insist they were 'loyal citizens, not intending to detract in the very least from the national war effort, in which a number of us are actively engaged'. Indeed, they were. The science and medical departments made major contributions to wartime production. Copland, his rough-hewn colleague Lyndhurst Giblin, and Kenneth Bailey all took up senior positions in Canberra, where they were to remain. Max Crawford would become First Secretary of the Australian embassy in the Soviet Union, George Browne of Education the chief Victorian censor, while Wadham would head the Rural Reconstruction Commission and Macmahon Ball of political science lead Radio Australia. Wright served along with Crawford on the Committee on National Morale (a prestigious policy unit 'consisting only of distinguished and disinterested minds' that reported to the prime minister); Donald Thomson, the anthropologist, returned to Arnhem Land to prepare an Aboriginal force to resist Japanese invaders. Latham resigned as Chancellor to lead a mission to Japan

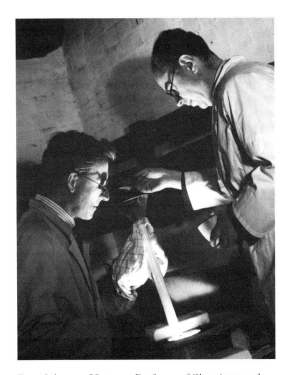

Ernst Johannes Hartung, Professor of Chemistry, and
his colleague Erich Heymann work on the wartime
production of optical munitions, using local sands in
pots of Australian clay.

in 1941, and was succeeded by Charles Lowe of the Supreme Court. Medley
himself became a member of the Australian Broadcasting Commission and
chair of the Services Education Council.

Enrolments rose rapidly in the first years of the war to 4600 in 1941, and
fell steeply after Japan entered the war to 3200 in the following year. Wartime
controls emptied the Arts Faculty while directing students into compressed
courses in medicine, science and engineering. Hitherto education had been a

responsibility of the states; now the Commonwealth set up a Universities Commission to determine quotas in these and other faculties of strategic significance. The largely deserted colleges were given over to Air Force personnel. All students trained in air raid precautions and first aid, and were required to contribute to the war effort during vacations; most picked fruit during the summer in the Goulburn Valley. Slit trenches and sandbags were scattered over the campus, and part of the grounds turned into vegetable gardens.

With the prospect of victory, the universities occupied a central position in post-war planning. Under the Commonwealth Reconstruction Training Scheme (CRTS), the government supported the studies of men and women returning from military service. From a few hundred in 1945 these students grew to 2600 in 1947, and by the following year the university's enrolment reached 9500. The CRTS students clustered in the professional courses but were not restricted to them, and those who returned to Arts were especially prominent in student life. Older, more independent and less deferential, they brought with them something of the impatience for change that associated wartime service with the goal of a new national and international order. These hopes found expression in the Labour Club, which dominated student politics with more than five hundred members, and within it the university branch of the Communist Party, which claimed at least one hundred activists.

The university responded as best it could to an influx of new students with novel expectations. Staff numbers doubled between 1945 and 1950, and among the recruits were distinguished intellectuals from Europe. Some had entered Australia as refugees from fascism, while others came after the war from the ravaged continental universities. Many of Melbourne's appointments were in new areas such as psychology, geography, fine arts, and the history and philosophy of science. Arts gained no fewer than five new chairs, as well as *Meanjin*, the literary quarterly, while commerce and law also benefited.

After the Second World War spread to the Pacific in 1941, ramparts of sandbags were erected around buildings to protect them from Japanese air-raids. (State Library of Victoria)

Gowned Labour Club members march by Trades Hall in 1947. Jenny Love and Peter Ryan (the only apostate) carry the banner, followed by Amirah Inglis, Ian Turner and Nita Murray-Smith. (courtesy Keith Benn)

This allocation was in part a necessity—it was difficult to recruit scientists, even more difficult to build and fit out laboratories—and in part a conscious choice: Medley was determined to balance the professional courses by strengthening liberal studies. Nor did his preference challenge national policy, which at this time affirmed the value of a university education across the range of disciplines. If science and engineering held the key to national security and industrial growth, medicine would improve the health of the population, the social sciences would make a similar contribution to public welfare, and the humanities preserve the civilised values of a modern nation. It was a scientist who proposed in 1944 that the university should offer the degree of Doctor of Philosophy for research students, but when the degree was established in the following year it was available in all fields of research. Arts led the way in the introduction of a fourth, honours year that was designed to extend the ordinary pass course into advanced studies.

These initiatives had special significance for the scientists, however, as they faced growing competition in their research mission from organisations such as the expanded Council for Scientific and Industrial Research and also from the new Australian National University (ANU). Founded in 1946, the ANU held itself aloof from the undergraduate Canberra University College (for which Melbourne retained academic responsibility). It was a research university, generously funded by the Commonwealth to conduct 'post-graduate study and research study', especially in 'subjects of national importance to Australia'. While Melbourne's thriving Medical Faculty might expect to withstand the ANU's fledgling School of Medical Research, and the new Research Schools of Pacific Studies and Social Sciences would foster national collaboration, the fourth Research School of Physical Sciences was a formidable rival.

Physics was at this time the most potent of the sciences, and the most expensive. The ANU lured Marcus Oliphant back from England to provide Australia with its own nuclear capacity, and supported him with a seemingly unlimited budget—while Melbourne's Department of Physics laboriously assembled a 'home-made cyclotron' that consumed the lion's share of the university's research funds. The enlistment of science in this and other projects of national significance called for linear increases of infrastructure

A corrugated-iron shed housing the physics annexe
laboratory was still in use in 1958.

capacity (hence the Snowy Mountains scheme) and a corresponding growth
of expertise. The fear that spurred the University of Melbourne to enhance its
provision for research was that the older universities would serve merely as
training institutions. Apart from the work on nuclear physics and cosmic ray
studies in Leslie Martin's Department of Physics, Sherborn Hills led research
in geomorphology and structural geology in the Department of Geology and
Oscar Tiegs led the Department of Zoology's advances in entomology.

The task of accommodating increased numbers of teachers, researchers
and students strained the university in the post-war period of reconstruction
and rationing. When teaching began 1946, the throng in Union House was
likened to Flinders Street during rush hour. With an acute national shortage
of building materials, the campus was littered with corrugated-iron huts.
Students boarded in the dilapidated terraces of a Carlton that was marked
down for slum clearance; an announcement that beer was on tap at Naugh-
ton's public bar would empty the Cafeteria. To ease the congestion, the university opened a new campus in 1947 on a former Air Force training camp at
Mildura, and for three years first-year students in medicine, dentistry, architecture and engineering lived and studied in this Mallee outpost.

The post-war Mildura campus, with water tower, lies marooned on a sparsely vegetated red-soil plain.

Students at their books outside their residence on the Mildura campus; mop, bucket and insect spray-can suggest the rudimentary conditions.

The Mildura branch was closed as the Commonwealth Reconstruction Training Scheme numbers dwindled. A corresponding decline of Commonwealth funding for these students revived the financial difficulties of Australian universities. In 1949 the Chifley government appointed a committee to consider further federal support. It completed its work in the following year and the new prime minister, Robert Menzies, accepted the recommendations. From 1951 the Commonwealth provided annual grants for the country's universities and also established a national system of scholarships that would cover fees and provide living allowances for several thousand students. These Commonwealth scholarships, along with the bursaries subsequently offered by the state Education Department (which again covered fees and living costs in return for three years of teaching in the rapidly expanding secondary school system) opened the university to a growing proportion of school-leavers. By removing the barriers of cost and leavening the undergraduate population with talent regardless of means, they did more to democratise higher education than any previous measure.

Menzies, a former student and future Chancellor of the University of Melbourne, was by no means enthusiastic for the idea of the university as a public institution serving national objectives laid out in government plans. Rather, he took a traditional view of the academy as a place of scholarship and preparation for the learned professions, which needed an appropriate measure of independence. 'A life is not rich which contains no cloisters', pronounced Menzies. Yet in 1952 the man he had appointed to lead the Australian Security and Intelligence Organisation (ASIO) assumed that the Commonwealth exercised control over at least one aspect of academic life. 'I am sure that you will readily appreciate', Colonel Charles Spry wrote to Menzies, 'the inadvisability of employing in any university lecturers who are likely to infest students with subversive doctrines'. ASIO had investigated the staff at the University of Melbourne, and found grounds for suspicion of no fewer than 63 of them. Some of the suspects had form as dissident public intellectuals: Max Crawford, Kathleen Fitzpatrick and Geoff Serle of history, Macmahon Ball of political science and Jim Cairns of economic history. The inclusion of others such as Zelman Cowen, a Professor of Law and future

Governor-General, is a measure of the fevered imagination of the country's custodians.

Public criticism of university staff was frequent and vituperative. In 1946 Albert Dunstan, a former premier, denounced Parkville's 'pink professors'. A Liberal member of the state parliament, Frederick Edmunds, embellished the alliterative epithets in the following year when he claimed that 'pink pundits and puce pedagogues' were defiling the university with their communist apologetics, contaminating students with teaching 'soggy with socialist prejudice'. Edmunds was especially critical of Max Crawford for his presidency of Australia–Soviet House, and of his colleague Manning Clark. The SRC and the honours class in history both wrote to the press to defend Crawford's integrity, and a group of students attended a meeting addressed by Edmunds at the Melbourne Town Hall to reply to his charges. They were denied the platform and denounced as a 'pack of dingoes'. Hence the song 'The Dingoes' Revenge' at the Labour Club revue later in the year, with Amirah Inglis (née Gust) and Nita Murray-Smith (Bluthal) as two innocent history students proclaiming:

> *We're red, we're red, he'd rather see us dead;*
> *Devoid of any intellect,*
> *The facts we learn are incorrect,*
> *Not giving Edmunds due respect,*
> *We're Varsity dingoes all.*

At this point Medley had the support of the state Labor government (led by John Cain senior) in his defence of the integrity of the staff. That support ended when a Liberal–Country Party coalition took office at the end of 1947. In 1948 the Minister for Education banned the screening at the university of films from communist countries. In 1949 the Victorian government appointed a royal commission into communism. Conducted by the Chancellor, Sir Charles Lowe, it rejected the claim that there was communist indoctrination at the university.

But in late 1949 Menzies led the Coalition parties to victory in a federal election and moved quickly to implement a ban on communism. After the

High Court struck down his Communist Party Dissolution Act, Menzies called a referendum and, at one of many university meetings on the issue, Professors Macmahon Ball, Cowen, Crawford and Wright all urged a 'no' vote. Lowe now objected to the use of university buildings for such meetings, and the Council once more was at odds with the staff on the limits of academic freedom. It was tense period. 'Pansy' Wright recalled receiving a telephone call one evening from a student working as a waiter at the Melbourne Club, who had overheard two senior university officers discussing over dinner how to dismiss the turbulent medical professor. What, asked the informant, should he do? Wright told him to go back to the table and listen carefully.

Sir John Medley—knighted in 1948—continued to defend intellectual freedom, but he was no longer Vice-Chancellor. Insisting that the university should be a hotbed and not a refrigerator, he announced his resignation in 1950. Medley's health was poor, for he lived on nerves and found conflict debilitating. A man of generous sympathies, Medley tempered high ideals with sensitivity to others and self-deprecating humour. His chief weakness was a reluctance to say no. It was unfortunate that his successor was even less resolute.

◊ ◊ ◊

George Paton, the new Vice-Chancellor, was appointed after wide advertisement of the post attracted no applicants. A Melbourne graduate, Rhodes Scholar and Professor of Jurisprudence since 1931, he was the first member of staff to lead the university since W. E. Hearn, another law professor, briefly held the office of Chancellor in 1886. Paton had served as Chairman of the Professorial Board and was a close friend of Medley, whose liberal values he shared; but he was less articulate and more cautious. The recent departure of the Registrar, John Foster, deprived him of an able administrator.

Indecisiveness was apparent almost immediately, when in the January of 1952 the Wilson Hall burnt down. This hall, the ceremonial centre of the university, had been built in 1882 with a bequest from a wealthy pastoralist, in

Fire gutted Wilson Hall on a hot afternoon in January 1952, and poor water pressure hampered the efforts of the fire brigade. Only a few portraits were saved.

the Gothic style to affirm the university's links with ancient seats of learning. The Council launched an appeal to restore the old hall, then changed its mind in favour of a cheaper modern building. The traditionalists protested, and twenty-five professors even threatened an injunction. Finally the modernists won, and a new Wilson Hall was constructed in brick on the bluestone footings of the old, and a large interior mural depicted a human figure reaching upwards for enlightenment from the strife and chaos below. Robin Boyd observed that the apparent victory of functionalist modernism had resulted in 'the crowning jewel of Australian featurism'. The acoustics were poor, and the glass curtain wall allowed the heat of the sun to shrivel the heavily robed academics as they performed the traditional degree ceremony.

Other buildings of the 1950s proclaimed the modernist ethos and betrayed its limitations. The sports centre, completed in 1956, featured an indoor swimming pool—appropriately so, since this was the year of triumph for Australian swimmers in the Melbourne Olympics, and the facility was built with a donation of £200 000 from Sir Frank Beaurepaire, the former freestyle champion. As athletics coach at the centre, the flamboyant Franz Stampfl achieved success with Ron Clark and Ralph Doubell, but the traditional pursuits of cricket and football retained their primacy.

International House, opened in 1958, again broke with tradition in design and operation. It was a hall of residence, starkly simple among the ornate villas of Royal Parade, and meant principally for the Asian students who were enrolled under the Colombo Plan of assistance to members of the British Commonwealth—though the policy of International House was to balance them with local residents. In the early 1950s Melbourne taught more Asian students than any other Australian university, and there were parallel attempts to promote Asian studies in languages, history, philosophy and politics. Yet Asian studies withered and Asian students did not return in large numbers until a less altruistic impulse, the need for fee income, concentrated the university's mind at the close of the century.

After repeated false starts, a library was completed in 1959. The Baillieu family had been donating funds for this sorely needed amenity since 1944, yet the library collection remained pitifully inadequate and the library staff were

Athol Shmith shot an exhibition of contemporary statuary in the new Wilson Hall in April 1957. The figure on the nearest pedestal averts its eyes from Douglas Annand's mural depiction of *A Search for Truth*.

treated as menial functionaries. The new Baillieu Library provided for 1000 reading places and a doubling of the current collection of 150 000 volumes. It was almost immediately swamped by 8000 daily readers and rapidly exhausted the storage capacity. Sydney University was already planning for double the reading places and three times as many books. Long overdue, the tragedy of Melbourne's library was that it was built too soon.

The mistake with the Architecture Building, many felt, was that it was built at all. The frustrations of its abrasive professor, Brian Lewis, illustrate the predicament of a smaller professional faculty, understaffed and banished to long-term occupancy of temporary huts. When he eventually obtained funding for a new building, Lewis insisted that it should be larger than the grant allowed and assembled material donations from industry into a strikingly unprepossessing structure. Lewis acknowledged that the result was 'a mutilated design with the cheapest finishes', but then he was never less than forthright and once declared he was as proud of his enemies as he was of his friends.

Another of the major buildings of this era, Biochemistry, also drew on a benefactor, Russell Grimwade. A pharmaceutical manufacturer, bibliophile and Council member, he had offered to contribute to the library but was diverted to this important discipline of the biological sciences. The first stage of an impressive scientific centre was opened in 1958, just off Royal Parade and opposite the Royal Melbourne Hospital and the Walter and Eliza Hall Institute. Another medical research institute, the Howard Florey Laboratories of Experimental Physiology, would follow a few years later. To the south of the hospital, the new Dental College was about to proceed, and near Biochemistry, a building for Microbiology. The Medical Faculty was mobilising with formidable strength and still had its eyes on the old hockey field in the south-west corner of the university grounds.

◊ ◊ ◊

Increased support from private benefactors suggested a greater appreciation of the university. A general appeal for funds, launched as part of the centenary

The high-rise buildings of the 1960s attached lecture theatres to exterior walls as functional motifs. This raked theatre in raw concrete was designed by Romberg and Boyd, architects of the Microbiology Building. (*University of Melbourne Gazette*, October 1965)

celebrations, raised £500 000. Those celebrations were originally planned for April 1955, one hundred years after the university had begun teaching, but were postponed to the following year. The fiftieth anniversary, similarly, had been set back to 1906 in the aftermath of Dickson's embezzlement. There would be no such laxity for the sesquicentenary, which anticipated both the laying of the foundation stone and the arrival of the first professors; it took the appointment of the first Council in April 1853 as the metrical moment.

Half a million pounds was an unprecedented addition to the university's income, and urgently needed to ease its chronic financial difficulties. A spurt of inflation in the early 1950s brought rising costs for capital works and salaries. The Staff Association, formed in 1944, emerged as an influential representative of academic interests. Melbourne's salary scales lagged behind those of Sydney, and the difficulties of attracting staff brought substantial increases of salaries in 1954 and 1955; but these were contingent on additional support from the state government, which closed its purse to further increases.

Lack of control over salaries was only part of the predicament of a public university dependent upon two paymasters with different priorities. The Commonwealth's annual grant was tied to specified levels of matching income, so that the university regularly pressed the Victorian government to increase its grant. The state Treasury usually provided an amount too small to maximise the Commonwealth's offer and too late to avert sudden cuts in expenditure that upset teaching arrangements and made long-term planning impossible. Steep increases in tuition fees, the only item of its income the university could control, were undercut by declining enrolments. Student numbers fell from a post-war peak of 9500 in 1948 to less than 7000 by 1954 (when Sydney surpassed Melbourne as the country's largest university). Yet the Faculty of Medicine was so concerned by the effect on teaching standards that it imposed quotas.

The deficiencies of the university's administration were exposed when the Commonwealth determined in 1957 on a comprehensive review of Australian universities. Unable to provide most of the information the review committee sought, the Registrar turned to the academic departments for estimates of student numbers. The group of professors who prepared Melbourne's submission were unable to establish priorities, let alone formulate a coherent plan. They identified deficiencies of resources, acknowledged the alarming failure rates that were an endemic feature of the haphazard postwar expansion, and drew on the rhetoric of the professor of philosophy to affirm the mission of the university as a place of higher learning.

The review, headed by the chair of the British University Grants Committee, Sir Keith Murray, made sharp observations on the quality of Australian universities. Its articulation of their proper role in national life gave an implicit rebuke to Melbourne's patrician submission. 'The days when universities could live in a world apart', the Murray Committee declared, 'if ever they truly existed, are long since over'. A university should provide 'a full and true education' to a very large number of citizens; it should contribute to knowledge both for practical purposes and for its own sake; and it should serve as a guardian of intellectual standards and freedom. Prime Minister Menzies implemented the recommendations for a permanent authority within the Commonwealth government that would co-ordinate the country's universities and provide triennial grants independently of the niggardly state governments. Melbourne's Professor of Physics, Leslie Martin, became the first chair of the Australian Universities Commission.

The Murray Committee's expansive redefinition of the university was a charter for growth. It released Canberra University College from the tutelage of Melbourne, though a consequent merger with the Australian National University imprisoned the College once more as a School of General Studies. It also confirmed that a second university would be established in Melbourne —for the existing university's enrolment had recovered to 7900 students by 1957 and would grow by a thousand in each subsequent year.

The Victorian government had proposed to the Murray Committee that the new university should have a technological emphasis (like the New South Wales University of Technology, established a decade earlier). But that university expanded to become the University of New South Wales in 1958, and the Murray Committee insisted that its Victorian counterpart should, from the outset, pursue applied sciences in conjunction with pure science and

In 1958 the *Herald* publicised the overcrowded conditions at the university. In a science laboratory, (left), students conduct experiments with apparatus crammed on to a bench.

In Babel, typists compete for space in an office building—but the two in the foreground were surely added for the occasion.

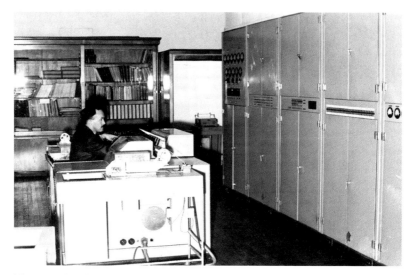

The Australian-built CSIR Mark 1 was among the first stored-program digital computers. In 1956 it was recommissioned in the Old Physics Building and renamed CSIRAC.

broaden the technological outlook with social sciences and the humanities. The legislation to establish the university in 1958 named it Monash, after an engineer who had also studied Arts and law, and its interim council established Arts, Commerce, Education and Law faculties as well as Engineering, Medicine and Science.

The new university, which began recruiting staff in 1960 and teaching in 1961, posed a formidable challenge to the old one. Beginning anew on fields at the edge of the city that were unmistakably green and often soggy, it was able to devise more efficient procedures, adopt more effective pedagogies and attract more adventurous academics. Monash perhaps underplayed its advantages. A provision of its statute, that 'the standard for graduation in the University shall be at least as high as prevails in the University of Melbourne', encouraged unhelpfully close comparison—the University of New South

Wales, by contrast, struck out more boldly and surpassed Sydney in its professional faculties. Even so, the more modernist, nationalist and democratic ethos at Clayton lured many of Parkville's best teachers and researchers. By the end of 1960 Melbourne had sixty unfilled vacancies, almost a tenth of its staff establishment.

By that time the full-time academic staff had grown to 576. There were more than fifty departments and still more professors—the Department of Mathematics had obtained a second chair in 1952, History in 1955. The old chair of engineering had been divided after the war into chairs of Civil, Mechanical and Electrical Engineering, with further departments of Metallurgy, Mining and Surveying. Economics and commerce now consisted of departments of Accounting, Commerce, Economic History, Economics and Economic Research, all with chairs, and a Department of Industrial Relations. Law resisted subdivision but had three established chairs, as did Dental Science. Science gained few new professors in the 1950s. Medicine, led from 1953 by Sydney Sunderland, obtained chairs in Pharmacology in 1954, then Medicine and Surgery in 1955. The provision of the latter clinical chairs had long been delayed; Sunderland would gather many more during his eighteen years as dean.

The growth in sub-professorial appointments was faster, and pregnant with implications. Before the war there had been one professor for every three other academics; now the ratio was approaching one to ten. The larger departments (Bacteriology, Biochemistry, Chemistry; Civil, Electrical and Mechanical Engineering; Economics, English, History, Mathematics, Pathology, Philosophy, Physics, Psychology) listed readers, senior lecturers, lecturer, tutors and demonstrators in a classification that confirmed the hierarchical nature of the university while it allowed for career progression. The large complement of research staff in the laboratory-based departments signalled their lines of growth.

Professors lost none of their authority. On the contrary, as permanent heads of their department they controlled its new appointments and promotions, supervised its teaching and research, determined its development. Collectively, through their exclusive membership of the Professorial Board, they governed academic life. In the absence of a professor, smaller departments such as History and Philosophy of Science, and free-standing schools such as Social Studies (both with female heads), needed influential patrons.

The most noticeable change in this enlarged structure was the growing administrative burden. The pre-war professor lectured, examined, kept up professional links, and sometimes pursued research. He might have assistance in his academic duties, but he wrote his own letters and kept his own accounts. Now he had a secretary but he was guiding a discipline, nurturing careers and managing an enterprise with endemic uncertainties of demand and supply. The university undertook to accept all qualified applicants and the student enrolment grew from 7000 in the middle of the decade to 10 279 in 1959 and 11 157 in 1960, yet the funding available to teach them was allocated in triennial grants that trailed some way behind. As Canberra saw it, Melbourne was over-enrolled by 10 per cent in 1960. All faculties except for architecture and law had followed medicine and set entry quotas.

There was little in an academic career that prepared professors for their tasks of leadership. A chair committee looked for an accomplished scholar with clear views on the development of the discipline and, so far as it could judge, an acceptable manner—for while Melbourne had abandoned its earlier practice of discerning the character of overseas applicants from photographic portraits, it still expected its professors to be gentlemen. An abrasive personality could wreak considerable damage, an indolent or ineffectual professorial head could reduce his discipline to a stagnant backwater.

The burden of administration hung heavily on some. Max Crawford, who had built a history department of unusual eminence, complained of the incessant demands—'writing the innumerable letters, attending the innumerable committees, planning policies, distributing scarce resources over plentiful demands'—that kept him from writing and teaching. Beset by ill health, Crawford became remote from later students, who would fleetingly experience the magic of his compellingly austere art. Other professors, Ian Maxwell in English, Macmahon Ball in political science, Zelman Cowen in law, Charles Moorhouse in engineering, were renowned for the way they professed their discipline, while still others were notoriously poor expositors.

Kathleen Fitzpatrick was renowned
for the grace of her delivery of lectures
in British history.

The classes that lodged in the memories of the students of the 1950s were more often conducted by teachers with fewer distractions. Kathleen Fitzpatrick, recalled for her 'wonderful mastery of the spoken and written word' by no less a wordsmith than Geoffrey Blainey, filled lecture theatres with precisely modulated presentations of Elizabethan and Puritan England. Yet she was passed over for the second chair in history.

Some teachers cultivated the reputation of a character, and some acquired celebrity regardless. Apocrypha gathered around 'Pansy' Wright. His physiology lectures challenged medical students accustomed to a systematic presentation of the curriculum, who now encountered a teacher in the Socratic mode and a showman of rasping jocularity. 'Pansy' would demonstrate principles and expect the class to apply them, scornful of convention, heedless of the effects on women students of his scatological jibes and heavy-handed misogyny. In tutorials, the medical playwright Jack Hibberd has recalled, 'he chain-smoked Turf (his skin seemed to exude tar), spoke pithily and stared glumly at fools'.

Note also the earlier response of a professor in the Arts Faculty when the members of his tutorial were struck dumb. 'All silent, and all damned', he rebuked them, and swept from the room. Academics were remarkably unconcerned by failure rates that by the end of the 1950s approached half the first-year intake to science. The dean of that faculty insisted that those who failed were manifestly not fit for science and should not have been taken in. In similar vein, an associate professor made an angry rebuttal of the criticisms levelled by the Murray Committee: 'There is not one shred of evidence of any relation between failure rates and the quality of teaching'. The university offered tuition of variable quality and it was up to the students to make what they could of it.

Student life was correspondingly self-sufficient. It had its own characters, some imitating and some challenging the models put before them. The post-war style had been marked by bohemian austerity—demob service apparel, student digs, the New Theatre, songbooks, progressive causes. This gave way to a new generation of school-leavers, less strident and at least outwardly more conformist—the first Miss University contest was held at the end of the 1940s. In summer the females wore the full, long skirts of the New Look, with flat shoes and pin-tucked blouses in summer, twinsets in winter. For men, Fletcher Jones trousers, tweed jackets and, in summer, national service military camps. A decade later and it was corduroy pants, viyella shirts, desert boots and duffle-coats.

Melbourne had relatively few part-time students to blur the boundaries of work and study. A high proportion of its student body came from the city's private schools, but the centre of gravity had shifted decisively south of Tin Alley. The Union provided a base for the clubs and societies that proliferated in this period. *Farrago*, the student newspaper, kept up a lively commentary on campus activity and sustained the larger cultural ambience of ideas,

Lunchtime in the Union House 'Caf', where the fare was plain but the conversation lively.

interests, causes and cosmopolitan tastes. Under the leadership of John Sumner and later Wal Cherry, the Union Theatre Repertory Company (later the Melbourne Theatre Company) flourished; cinema screenings in the Union Theatre spawned the Melbourne Film Festival. In nearby Carlton there was the Bug House cinema, Jimmy Watson's wine bar, and the restaurants and coffee lounges of post-war Italian migrants.

The Cold War sapped the fervour of the Labour Club. By 1949 the Liberal Club, which included future parliamentarians such as Ivor Greenwood, Alan Hunt and Alan Missen, had broken left-wing control of the SRC. By 1951 Ian Maxwell, a former member of an earlier and more Liberal Club, was reciting Milton and Kathleen Fitzpatrick was recounting the Putney Debates as oblique commentaries on the referendum to ban communism. By 1953 Barry Humphries was staging his Dadaist stunts. An assault on a fake blind man in front of appalled train-travellers; disguising himself as a filthy scavenger to pluck chicken and champagne from a garbage bin by a bus stop; spooning up Heinz's Russian salad from a city pavement—these were calculated affronts to conventional sensibility, as was his languid dandyism. The performances revived the provocation of town by gown that had previously been encoded in the commencement procession, but in a more consciously aesthetic mode that emphasised the retreat from political engagement.

Engagement persisted nevertheless, both in the revisionist circles that charted a new course for social democracy (this generation of future Labor politicians included John Button, John Cain, Michael Duffy, Barry Jones, Joan Kirner and Race Mathews) and in the active Christian groups that proclaimed the social gospel. The Student Christian Movement and the Newman Society were both prominent, as indeed were the equally evangelical Rationalists and Fabians. Students contested capital punishment, censorship, curtailment of civil liberties. They raised funds for Aboriginal scholarships, condemned apartheid. The Immigration Reform Group was formed out of these humanitarian concerns. Its publication in 1960 of the pamphlet *Control or Colour Bar* heralded the end of the White Australia policy.

For those who took up these causes, the university was no longer a place removed from public controversy but a special place that fostered their engagement. Few restrictions remained on campus political activity. Though debate was often robust and stratagems dubious, the activity was shaped by academic norms of respect for evidence, critical reflection and reasoned argument. The stakes were high because participants were convinced that ideas mattered, and that by virtue of their intellectual vocation they could act on the social conscience.

With this idea of the liberal university came the insistence on freedom from outside interference. The principle of academic freedom was now established, though not always observed. The celebrated case of Sydney Sparkes Orr, dismissed from the University of Tasmania on a charge of immorality, aroused protest because there was disturbing evidence that the Tasmanian government and judiciary were colluding in a denial of natural justice. Orr was a notoriously difficult man—but then, martyrs are seldom congenial. The case particularly exercised Melbourne academics because he had been a lecturer at this university before taking the chair of Philosophy there. 'Pansy' Wright took up the cause, along with the Melbourne Staff Association, and suffered Orr's ingratitude for nearly a decade before a settlement of sorts was finally reached.

Melbourne experienced its own staff controversy in 1961 when its most abrasive Cold Warrior alleged a communist conspiracy in the Department of Social Studies. Frank Knopfelmacher, an ex-communist refugee from Czechoslovakia and a lecturer in the Department of Psychology, surprised no one with his obsessive witch-hunt. The shock came when the history professor Max Crawford, himself a victim of similar allegations in the past, wrote in the *Bulletin* that he had witnessed the campaign to take control of Social Studies. Crawford's wife was head of the department and he turned a dispute over its conduct into accusations of subversion that he took up with the national security agency, which it in turn passed on to Knopfelmacher and the editor of the *Bulletin*. A university inquiry dismissed the idea of a communist plot and ignored the anti-communist one.

The Council and officers of the university treated this controversy as they had dealt with issues of management during the 1950s—reactively. They expanded the staff in response to post-war demand, and then imposed economies when enrolments fell away. They embarked on research as an essential component of the modern university, but struggled to sustain it. They built when opportunity allowed, on a piecemeal basis. Such improvisation no longer sufficed in the following decade. A large cohort of students arrived with greater expectations. The affectionate nickname 'the Shop', a place that supplied credentials, had little meaning to these fortunate baby-boomers, for they assumed their educational entitlements, and jobs were freely available regardless of qualifications. With a sometimes self-indulgent idealism, they expected more of the university than it offered them. The government, which met the growing cost of an expanded system of higher education, became increasingly exasperated by its apparent failure. The pressures of the 1960s found Melbourne wanting.

The guiding principle of the public university extended the commercial metaphor of the Shop from the single customer to the nation at large. The benefits of university study to the individual student, argued the Committee on the Future of Tertiary Education in Australia in 1964, were 'only a fraction of the benefits accruing to society'. Hence education should be seen as 'a form of national investment in human capital' that government made for the common good. But public investment was a finite resource and this committee, chaired by Sir Leslie Martin, the Chairman of the Australian Universities Commission, was charged with advising the prime minister how the Commonwealth could avoid uncontrolled rises in the cost of tertiary education.

It did so by drawing a sharper distinction between universities and other institutions. Martin, a physicist, was insistent on the purity of the university as a place of intellectual inquiry where teaching and research were inseparable. If applied research was needed it should be done elsewhere, along with the narrowly vocational training needed to remedy the shortages of skilled personnel. From this redefinition came the binary divide that prevailed for the next two decades between the universities and the technical and teachers' colleges (or the colleges of advanced education, as they became), the one sector affirming the research–teaching nexus and funded accordingly, the other assigned a subordinate role. The government accepted the distinction, but rejected Martin's call for his Universities Commission to become a Tertiary Education Commission. The result was an unregulated binary system with perennial demarcation disputes.

The binary divide confirmed the directions taken by Melbourne. While the Murray Committee was deliberating, the Medical Faculty had seized the opportunity to increase its intake from 160 to 240 students per year. With this expansion the university's building fund was sequestered for a new Medical School so that the faculty could complete its move to the south-west corner of the campus. New chairs were created, eighty staff added. As other faculties came to see that the expansion would be at the expense of their own plans, a professor of history told the Professorial Board, *'nous sommes trahis'*.

Other buildings were raised on the remaining empty spaces of a campus that seemed constantly under construction. The additions were tall, rectilinear structures that paid little heed to older forms and purposes. With sheer facades that rose above any natural shade, they were aligned on an east–west axis to cope with the summer sun, unlike the earlier buildings that ran north to south. The starkly functionalist Economics and Commerce Building cut into the row of professor's houses, and the twelve-story Redmond Barry Building was a remarkable affront to the classical taste of its namesake. To name the administrative centre, completed in 1969, after Raymond Priestley was even less appropriate. The building closed off the vista from Wilson Hall to his beloved Union; its elevation on two legs merely buffeted all who walked through the wind-swept undercroft. The removal of the Vice-Chancellor from the Quadrangle to the highest of its nine floors increased his isolation, and the eight floors below indicated the rapid growth of the central administration.

◊ ◊ ◊

The administration had grown to provide an increased range of services to larger numbers of staff and students, and to manage the operation of an increasingly complex organisation. Decision-making was vested in a labyrinth of committees, resource allocation controlled by the Council, and the two principal officers, the Vice-Chancellor and the Registrar, seemed unable to reconcile academic and financial priorities. The appointment of a Deputy Vice-Chancellor (Sherborn Hills of geology) in 1962 provided little relief to a Vice-Chancellor who was loath to depute. The university dealt with the regular deficits caused by persistent over-enrolment with temporary cuts, in the forlorn belief that the Australian Universities Commission would at last

George Paton at the opening of the Redmond Barry Building in 1960. The
Chancellor, Sir Arthur Dean (left), and an inscrutable Premier, Henry
Bolte, sit under the canopy behind him.

A drawing of the north face of the administration building, completed in
1969. The Vice-Chancellor and his staff occupied panelled offices on the top
floor. Though strictly the tenth floor, the 'Ninth Floor' became the
colloquialism for decisions made on high.

bring relief. Yet with the expansion of medicine and the re-establishment in 1963 of the Faculty of Veterinary Science, Melbourne had committed itself to the two disciplines that were most expensive to teach just as the Commonwealth was scrutinising its grants to the universities.

At the end of 1963 the resourceful Dr Phillip Law (who had taught in the Physics Department before turning to the Antarctic) persuaded Council that an administrative review was necessary. In early 1964 the state Auditor-General uncovered serious problems in the university's financial procedures. Later in the same year the Staff Association warned of a serious decline in morale and expressed lack of confidence in the university management. The Students' Representative Council followed with a report to Council on the effect on teaching of overcrowded classes and inadequate facilities. By the end of the year Phillip Law's committee submitted its first report to Council and recommended the appointment of a senior officer to take charge of financial policy, buildings and grounds. It was fortunate that Ray Marginson, a commerce graduate with extensive experience in the Commonwealth Public Service, moved quickly in the new post of Vice-Principal to impose order. The Victorian parliament's Public Accounts Committee had followed the Auditor-General's report with a stringent examination of the university's senior administrators. The report would have been far more damning if Marginson had not moved quickly to deal with many of its recommendations.

The Commonwealth was less merciful. The 1966 report of its Australian Universities Commission brushed aside Melbourne's arguments for a larger grant in the next triennium. John Gorton, the Oxford-educated Minister for Education, believed the commission had been too generous, and cut the grant. While the state government provided some relief, its sympathy for the university was approaching exhaustion. Memories of protest against a hanging in 1962, when students had let down the tyres of the Premier's car, still rankled. A subsequent demonstration in 1966 against the visiting American President brought backbench criticism of the 'undesirable, unkempt, unwashed, uncultured and unprofitable people in our universities'. One government member insisted the fault lay with the lax Vice-Chancellor: 'The

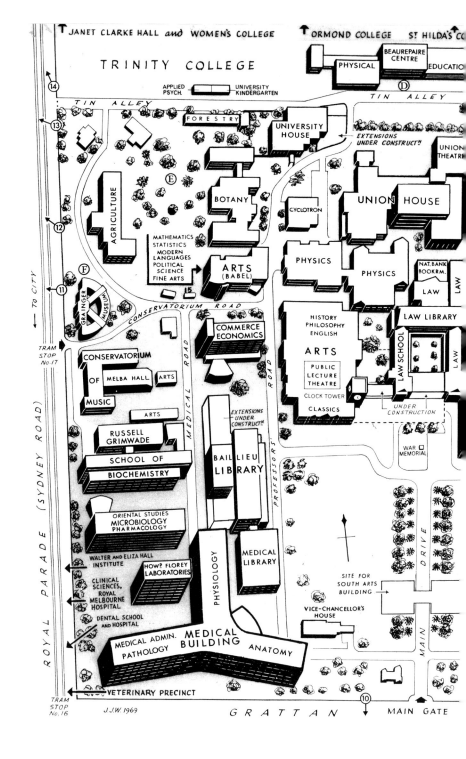

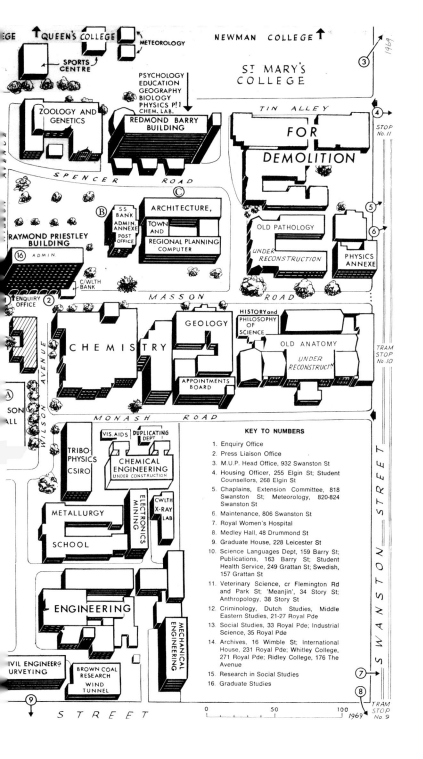

QUEEN'S COLLEGE
METEOROLOGY
NEWMAN COLLEGE
SPORTS CENTRE
S.T MARY'S COLLEGE
1969

PSYCHOLOGY
EDUCATION
GEOGRAPHY
BIOLOGY
PHYSICS P.t I
CHEM. LAB.

ZOOLOGY AND GENETICS

REDMOND BARRY BUILDING

TIN ALLEY

FOR DEMOLITION

STOP No. 11

SPENCER ROAD

ARCHITECTURE,

S.S BANK
ADMIN. ANNEXE
POST OFFICE

TOWN AND REGIONAL PLANNING COMPUTER

RAYMOND PRIESTLEY BUILDING

ADMIN.

OLD PATHOLOGY

UNDER RECONSTRUCTION

PHYSICS ANNEXE

C/WLTH BANK

ENQUIRY OFFICE

MASSON ROAD

HISTORY and PHILOSOPHY OF SCIENCE

GEOLOGY

OLD ANATOMY

UNDER RECONSTRUCT.N

CHEMISTRY

APPOINTMENTS BOARD

TRAM STOP No. 10

WILSON AVENUE

SON ALL

MONASH ROAD

VIS. AIDS
DUPLICATING DEPT.

TRIBO-PHYSICS
CSIRO

CHEMICAL ENGINEERING
UNDER CONSTRUCTION

ELECTRONICS MINING

METALLURGY

CWLTH X-RAY LAB

SCHOOL

ENGINEERING

MECHANICAL ENGINEERING

CIVIL ENGINEER.G SURVEYING

BROWN COAL RESEARCH
WIND TUNNEL

STREET

SWANSTON STREET

TRAM STOP No. 9

1969

KEY TO NUMBERS

1. Enquiry Office
2. Press Liaison Office
3. M.U.P. Head Office, 932 Swanston St
4. Housing Officer, 255 Elgin St; Student Counsellors, 268 Elgin St
5. Chaplains, Extension Committee, 818 Swanston St; Meteorology, 820-824 Swanston St
6. Maintenance, 806 Swanston St
7. Royal Women's Hospital
8. Medley Hall, 48 Drummond St
9. Graduate House, 228 Leicester St
10. Science Languages Dept, 159 Barry St; Publications, 163 Barry St; Student Health Service, 249 Grattan St; Swedish, 157 Grattan St
11. Veterinary Science, cr Flemington Rd and Park St; 'Meanjin', 34 Story St; Anthropology, 38 Story St
12. Criminology, Dutch Studies, Middle Eastern Studies, 21-27 Royal Pde
13. Social Studies, 33 Royal Pde; Industrial Science, 35 Royal Pde
14. Archives, 16 Wimble St; International House, 231 Royal Pde; Whitley College, 271 Royal Pde; Ridley College, 176 The Avenue
15. Research in Social Studies
16. Graduate Studies

0   50   100
1969

position is hopeless with Professor Paton'. The omission of his title (he had been Sir George since 1957) emphasised the disrespect.

An ill-timed press release completed the Vice-Chancellor's discomfiture. In early 1967 the university announced that the cuts in Commonwealth funding would cause a disastrous curtailment of postgraduate training. Gorton sent the new chair of the Universities Commission—he had decided that the academic composition of the commission fostered too cosy a relationship with the importunate universities, and replaced Sir Leslie Martin with Lenox Hewitt, a senior Treasury official—for a meeting with Paton. The mandarin turned the meeting into an inquisition, and the nonplussed Vice-Chancellor failed to provide much of the information Hewitt demanded. Attempts at mollification merely aggravated his ire: at a city luncheon with officers of the university, Hewitt thumped the table as he castigated their organisation's waste, inefficiency and lack of accountability. Attempts to bypass him were no more effective. Sir Robert Menzies, who had become Chancellor after his retirement from government, was rebuffed in overtures to Gorton. On a visit to London in 1968 he confided to a former student and future dean that 'when I was prime minister I could get through anything that I wanted on universities, now I am Chancellor of the Melbourne University I find that it is broke and cannot do anything about it'.

Authority falls away from a former prime minister and also from a valedictory vice-chancellor. At the end of 1966 it was announced that Paton would retire early in 1968. His successor, David Derham, had left a chair in the Law Faculty to become foundation Dean at Monash, and in the interval between his appointment and arrival the university continued to drift. Student numbers stabilised at just below 14 000 while postgraduate numbers reached 1000. By this time the participation rate was moving towards 10 per cent of all Victorians of university age, so that the social origins of Melbourne's student body were less exclusive. With a ratio of eleven students for every member of staff, the university would seem able to provide adequate

Previous facing pages: Map 4 The university grounds in 1969, showing how the new high-rise buildings were squeezed onto the campus.

tuition; yet student dissatisfaction grew. Overcrowding was one complaint, publicised by overnight occupations of the Baillieu Library. Poor teaching was another, signalled by showers of paper darts directed at some notoriously incapable lecturers. Efforts to improve teaching led in 1962 to the establishment of a University Teaching Office, which developed under the leadership of Barbara Falk into the Centre for the Study of Higher Education—but some of those most in need of her assistance did not seek it.

Students also complained of the lack of personal contact: 'I get the impression that these people are on a pedestal more or less, and I think it would be terrific for staff–student relations if they'd come down a little bit'. Their teachers, on the other hand, worried that so many undergraduates entered university with ill-formed expectations and seemed so unaffected by the academic experience. A sociological study of Arts and science undergraduates in 1967 suggested that nearly half took no part in extracurricular activities. Undergraduates themselves bemoaned the malaise of student apathy with such insistence that the condition was difficult to discern. The Orientation Handbook for that year listed 120 clubs and societies in addition to the sporting clubs. Many of them issued roneoed broadsheets, produced little magazines, chalked walls and footpaths to advertise their lunchtime meetings and off-campus rallies. The distance between staff and students was shrinking as lecturers abandoned gowns and first names replaced surnames in classes.

Campus life was visibly changing. Indian shift or miniskirt and coloured tights, denim jeans, screen-printed teeshirts, leather jackets, shoulder-length hair topped with a Bob Dylan cap or Che Guevara beret, provided a repertoire of student chic. *Farrago* went from letterpress to offprint, using the new format to striking effect. A strong musical influence fused the popular and exotic, the plangent harmony of the folksong and the driving rhythm of the amplified guitar. These cultural forms were not peculiar to the university— they were aspects of a more general youth culture—but activists on campuses around the world assembled them into an iconoclastic counter-culture.

The student protest movement came late to Melbourne. At other universities criticism of Australia's military participation in the Vietnam War

The loans desk at the Bailllieu Library, 1961. Taken just two years after the library opened, the distraught manner of the man on the right suggests that services were already under pressure.

swelled into support for Third World liberation struggles. The decision in 1966 to send conscripts to Vietnam brought open defiance. Monash took the lead with the stridently confrontational tactics of its radicals and the heavy-handed disciplinary measures of its administration. At Melbourne the Students' Representative Council retained authority. There were few mass rallies and Sir George Paton imposed few restrictions. But two months after his retirement in May 1968, students took to the streets in Paris, London, New York and other cities. A new and far less lenient vice-chancellor had come to deal with more provocative unrest. It was just one of the challenges he faced.

How Worldly?

The new Vice-Chancellor took up his duties early in 1968. An appreciation of Melbourne's strengths and weaknesses was sharpened by the four years he had spent at Monash, three of them as a member of the Australian Universities Commission. He was well aware of Melbourne's financial difficulties and administrative deficiencies, its poor staff morale and low public standing. He was also acutely conscious of the vulnerability of the civic university, established and funded by government on behalf of the community at a time of rancorous conflict. A university served its community, in part by allowing for the exploration of contentious ideas, and its overriding commitment must be 'the acquisition and dissemination of knowledge beyond mere reference to any needs of particular times or places'. The university therefore required a substantial measure of autonomy, and this in turn depended on a 'capacity to manage its own affairs' that was in need of urgent rehabilitation.

To this task David Derham brought a lawyer's passion for order and proper procedure. He also brought a new Registrar, Brigadier A. T. J. Bell, formerly chief of staff of Southern Command, who reinforced the peremptory tone of the new regime. Derham was a man of strong opinions bluntly expressed, patient and considerate of individual frailty, but stiff and forbidding in his official capacity. He lacked rapport with the demonstrative student enthusiasms and was visibly uncomfortable with students *en masse*. A spontaneous word or gesture might have defused the hostility that isolated him

The newly appointed Vice-Chancellor, David Derham,
1966. 'The task of Vice-Chancellor', he commented, 'is
the administration of a very complicated corporation'.
(Media and Publications)

from the student body over the next few years; instead he sallied forth grimly
from the Raymond Priestley Building as a paladin among the heathens.

Derham's most pressing task was to restore the university's solvency, and
to this end he set out to reduce some of its commitments. Thirty years earlier
Raymond Priestley had noted the vulnerability of Melbourne to the importunate demands of impractical enthusiasts for vocational training courses made
up of 'practical subjects', and the 'consequent starvation' of 'the more fundamental studies'. These courses were academically attenuated (they usually
offered a diploma rather than a degree) and made little contribution to the
university's research, and Melbourne had accumulated more of them by the
1960s than any other Australian university. Derham culled some (such as
journalism) and turned others (such as Social Studies) into graduate programs. Training in musical performance ostensibly went down to the
Victorian College of the Arts, leaving composition and musicology to the
Faculty of Music, though in practice the demarcation remained incomplete.

It was soon apparent that further economies would be necessary. In mid-
1969 Derham became aware that the Commonwealth's grant for the 1970–72

triennium would offer little relief. Concerned that a further round of *ad hoc* cuts would do serious damage, he decided that a complete review of funding was required and divested himself of all other duties to undertake it. Over the next ten weeks he assembled an inventory of the resources available to every one of the university's ninety departments, analysed their staff numbers and workloads, met with their heads to identify savings and ascertain priorities. From this Domesday survey a new budget was constructed that enabled the university to absorb the rigours of the next triennial grant without stultifying some important initiatives. Beyond that necessary expedient, it reformed the organisation and management of the university at all levels—not just departments but faculties, the university officers and the Council.

The exercise was described as basic budgeting, because its immediate purpose was to provide each department with a budgetary allocation on a new basis. With their revised level of funding, departments acquired greater responsibility for expenditure. Previously they had made requests for new staff to the central administration and thereby built up a complement of appointments; the efficacy of a head's pleading as well as the financial vagaries of the university would determine whether an established position was refilled or left vacant when its incumbent departed. Now this confusing backlog was swept away and departments were expected to live within their means. Derham insisted that a proportion of future appointments should be non-tenured (to preserve flexibility) and that a vacancy at a senior level should normally revert to a lectureship (for this was a necessary condition of promotion on merit and without quotas).

The basic budget having been determined as an emergency measure, responsibility for future funding was given to a Central Budgets Committee established as a joint committee of the Council and the Professorial Board. The device of the joint committee closed the gap between a governing body made up largely of lay members, and the principal academic forum. The Budgets Committee moved towards a formula based on the cost of teaching students in various disciplines to determine its allocations, and made them to the faculties on an annual basis. Each faculty established its own budget committee to distribute the funds among the constituent departments. While most of the dozen faculties exercised their new power tentatively, it invested them with new significance. With the exception of medicine, the large, multi-disciplinary faculties had hitherto operated as loose confederations of fiercely independent baronies; henceforth their fortunes were inseparable. For the time being, however, they continued to be governed feebly by deans who were temporary heads of state. Some coveted greater influence in university government, and the Dean of Veterinary Science hosted a dinner at the Zoo that gave birth in 1972 to a Committee of Deans. Derham allowed it no powers.

He was unable to prevent the growth of collective authority at other levels. Disturbed by the irregularities that his close inspection during the basic budget visitations made painfully apparent, the Vice-Chancellor arranged for the preparation of a Staff Procedure Guide. The consequent codification of entitlements and duties removed many of the anomalies that had flourished in the years of unplanned growth. It laid down a sharp separation between academic and general staff, and a clear structure for the latter. It also removed many of the discretions previously exercised by professorial heads of departments. Departmental heads were now bound by appointment procedures; promotions were determined by an independent committee; disputes could be taken for adjudication; there were regular departmental meetings to transact business, and—by far the most significant change—the office was now open to any senior member. The god professor no longer ruled by divine right; he derived his authority from his subjects. By 1978 even the university's house of lords bowed to the change, now that it contained so many commoners, and altered its name from the Professorial Board to the Academic Board.

Two processes were at work here. One was the formulation of rights and responsibilities as the university assumed the routines of a large bureaucratic organisation. The other was the demand for a more democratic university. The first provided clearly defined rules, predictable outcomes, stability; the second operated as a force for change, experiment and conflict. It was not easy to reconcile the collegial principle inherent in the idea of the university as a scholarly community with the delegated responsibilities embedded in the operation of a statutory corporation. It was far more difficult to accommodate the enlarged democracy demanded in the aftermath of May 1968.

The democracy that the student radicals espoused went far beyond representation in departmental meetings and university committees. They spoke of a 'participatory democracy' transacted in open forums, and they sought to democratise the university as an agent of social change. The new orientation was apparent in the appearance at Melbourne, late in 1968, of the Students for a Democratic Society (SDS), formed out of a grouping of student clubs opposed to conscription and the Vietnam war, and with a breakaway element from the Labour Club in the forefront. The Labour Club had been agitating against conscription and war through the usual forms of lunchtime talks and city marches. The SDS leaders, Harry Van Moorst and Michael Hamel-Green, argued for a more forceful strategy of direct action. Over the summer of 1968–69 they defied a by-law of the Melbourne City Council that prohibited the distribution of leaflets on city streets, refused to pay fines and served prison terms. Growing protest brought much publicity and revocation of the by-law.

The Students for a Democratic Society soon applied the same tactics to the university. Harry Van Moorst used the University Open Day in May 1969 to collect funds for medical aid to the National Liberation Front of Vietnam, and approached the Governor for a donation. The Vice-Chancellor's testy reprimand seemed akin to the Lord Mayor's prohibition, especially when Derham told Council that as the collection appeared to contravene the law, university officers were required to stop it. SDS went further later in the year when a meeting of students voted to use the university as a sanctuary for draft resisters: in a dawn raid in 1971 the police would batter down the doors of the Union House where four of them had taken refuge among hundreds of supporters.

In these and other skirmishes, student radicals asserted a new relationship between the university and the community. They used it as a sanctuary, a recruiting ground and a theatre. They criticised its links with government and industry, and they subjected its curriculum and pedagogy to fundamental critique. They wanted the university to serve society, but as a seedbed of liberation. These uses alarmed many members of the university beside the Vice-Chancellor, because their partisan nature seemed to threaten academic freedom. Student activists, on the other hand, took this concern as mere

Harry Van Moorst at the Vietnam War victory
celebrations in 1975. Diminutive, self-effacing
and intransigent, he became synonymous
with Melbourne's student protest movement.
(photograph by John Ellis)

obfuscation of the senior academics' patent lack of sympathy for their ideals.
An influential prophet of the New Left had advised that 'repressive tolerance'
was a device authorities used to stifle dissent. The tactic of the radicals was to
demonstrate this by calculated acts of confrontation.

The issue came to a head in 1970 when the university refused admission
to Albert Langer, a famously confrontational activist from Monash. Demanding repeal of the admissions statute, a group of students invaded a meeting of

the Professorial Board. Disciplinary charges were laid against thirty-two of them. This in turn brought an occupation of the Priestley Building to demand that the disciplinary proceedings be conducted openly, and when the Council dismissed a protest against 'the high-handed and arbitrary dismissal of student concerns', its meetings also were placed under siege. A subsequent mass protest in May 1971, locked out of the Priestley Building, resorted to a 'lock-in', and mounted police were about to be used when the protestors allowed the staff to leave. This action brought further disciplinary charges, but by now the Vice-Chancellor's obduracy was attracting criticism. Two law professors refused to serve on the disciplinary tribunal. The departure of Derham on an overseas trip allowed for a face-saving compromise, and the charges were dropped.

It was in this context that the university unlocked its doors to student representatives. Legislation in 1968 had added the president of the Students' Representative Council to the two other elected students on the university Council. The 1970 regulations governing departmental meetings provided for student membership. Following the May 1971 protest, Council decided on a review of university government, and surprisingly allowed it to be conducted by a working group of staff and student representatives. It came up with the idea of a permanent consultative body, the University Assembly, consisting of no less than 114 members elected from the students, academics and administrators. The involvement of the last of these was long overdue since the general staff, as they were styled, brought an intimate familiarity with the university's organisational strengths and weaknesses. Chaired by Davis McCaughey, the Master of Ormond College, and described by its first secretary as an 'exercise in open government', the Assembly provided a monthly forum with indeterminate powers as well as working groups on a host of schemes for improvement. Derham abhorred the experiment, while radicals regarded it as a palliative. Yet in its early years the Assembly achieved a good deal.

In its practical, reforming zeal, as well as in its inclusive procedures, the Assembly caught the new national mood. The election of a Labor government in 1972, after more than two decades of Coalition rule, brought rapid change to the political landscape. The withdrawal of Australian troops from Vietnam and the abolition of conscription removed the most potent factor in student protest. Ronald Henderson had already left the university's Institute of Applied Economic and Social Research to head an Australian Commission of Inquiry into Poverty, which now began preparing the blueprint of a comprehensive system of social welfare. Colleagues in the Institute devised Medibank. His friend Dick Downing, who held a Research Chair in Economics, became Chairman of the Australian Broadcasting Commission, as part of a cultural renaissance that helped Melbourne's young playwrights, film-makers and writers to reach a national audience. More than one campus activist became a ministerial adviser.

The university had submitted its proposals for the 1973–75 triennium to the Australian Universities Commission before the change of government, and fared well in the recommendations of its new chair, Peter Karmel. Following Whitlam's accession to office, Karmel added a Schools Commission to his responsibilities as the government embarked on comprehensive support of private as well as public schools. In 1973 the Commonwealth announced that it would assume full responsibility for funding universities. Student fees were abolished, and living allowances introduced. Derham saw dangers in this cornucopia. Universities would have to operate 'within the boundaries set by the generous and benevolent grants made by one national government', but if that government ceased to be generous and benevolent, there would be no protection from its interference.

The removal of fees and provision of living allowances allowed many who had previously been unable to afford tertiary education to make good their loss. By 1975, 40 per cent of students in Australian universities were over twenty-three years old. The 'mature-age students', as they were styled, were most numerous on the newer campuses, but there were enough of them at Melbourne to dilute further its exclusive 'finishing school' atmosphere. Women, who were the most disadvantaged in their educational opportunities, were the principal beneficiaries, yet when they arrived at the university they encountered patterns of sexual inequality of startling clarity. In 1974 more females than males completed secondary education and 42 per cent of

Priscilla Kincaid-Smith was appointed to a personal
chair in 1975, chaired the Australian Medical
Association and served as president of the World
Medical Association. (Media and Publications)

students at the university were women, but there was not one female professor. The first would be Priscilla Kincaid-Smith, appointed to a personal
chair in Medicine in 1975; the second, Sister Margaret Manion, who became
Professor of Fine Arts in 1979, and the third was Nancy Millis of Microbiology in 1982. There were legions of women at the level of tutor, demonstrator or research assistant, many with decades of service, but a remarkable
paucity of senior female academics. Hence the university's Staff and Distaff
Association operated as a support group for the wives of newly arrived
members of staff.

By the end of the 1960s, interest in the luncheons and tea parties of the
Staff and Distaff Association was waning as the distaff pursued their own
careers. The annual Miss University competition also disappeared at this
juncture. It had lapsed in the early 1950s, revived with an emphasis on raising
funds for charity, only to decline into an unruly spectacle. Picketing of beauty
contests was one of the activities that brought the revived feminist move-

ment to public attention. University women, mainly postgraduates, formed consciousness-raising groups in 1971 and helped organise a Women's Liberation Conference. In 1972 Germaine Greer, a celebrated student of the late 1950s, returned to promote her book, *The Female Eunuch*, and in the same year a group of Melbourne graduates formed the Women's Electoral Lobby.

The chief concern of the women who returned to study was the lack of provision for mothers with pre-school children. There was the (Lady) Alice Paton kindergarten that catered primarily for the children of staff, and a more recent Family Club nursery and kindergarten with a hopelessly long waiting list. A Childcare Action Group Council publicised the need for greater provision, but the Vice-Chancellor was loath to accept the commitment without funding from the Australian Universities Commission. His prevarication resuscitated the protest movement.

Harry Van Moorst had been elected to Council in 1973 on a forthright undertaking that he would use it as a 'battle front' and not 'an elitist club where it is desirable to suck up and be nice to the powers that be'. When Council rejected a motion that the university accept responsibility for the provision of child-care, Van Moorst led an invasion of its meeting on 6 May 1974. Police cleared the Council Chamber, arresting fourteen students, but on the next day much larger numbers gathered to resume action. The Priestley Building was again blockaded, and the Council Chamber reoccupied. Students turned the portrait of Sir Robert Menzies, the former Chancellor, to the wall and scrawled the words 'Child Care Now' on its back. They set up a child-minding centre in an adjoining room, and operated it for three days to make their point. While Council pressed court charges and thirteen students were fined, it also established child-care centres.

◊ ◊ ◊

Of these troubled times a story is told—it is probably apocryphal but no less instructive for that—of another episode of direct action. On a hot summer afternoon in 1971, building workers on a construction site to the south of the

Quadrangle were pouring concrete, and to keep it from setting too quickly they played water from hoses onto the formes. From cooling each other in the spray it was a short step to directing streams at passers-by. Suddenly they were confronted by a choleric man in a suit who demanded to know what they were doing. They looked at him, they looked at each other, and they turned the hose on him. Thanks to the foresight of his predecessor, the Vice-Chancellor was able to retreat to his adjacent residence.

Of all the decisions taken by the university at this time, the construction of this underground carpark appeared to student radicals to express most starkly the mistaken priorities of its administration. It was a staff facility, for students had been unable to bring cars onto the campus for more than a decade, and in any case the activists were pedestrians who lived communally in local terrace houses. It seemed to remove the last open space where students could sit in summer, play games in winter and court in spring— as late as 1963 the Registrar sent junior staff to order couples to separate. It was built under the guidance of the university's Master Planner, as part of a comprehensive landscaping of the campus that puritans regarded as a costly extravagance. Few would now dispute the merits of the South Car Park, which has preserved the area it occupies from further development while its subterranean forest of hyperbolic paraboloid shells is praised as forming the university's most impressive interior space. Few would regret the Master Plan, which has retrieved the amenity and beauty of an over-crowded campus.

The late 1960s and early 1970s saw the exhaustion of space for additional buildings. The triennial grants of the Australian Universities Commission, so parsimonious in their provision for teaching and research, allowed generously for capital works. Where to put them? The colleges blocked expansion north, while Parkville to the west was already sacrosanct, and urban conservation groups were resisting encroachment east into Carlton. A new building for the Arts Faculty, named after John Medley, was placed at the southern entrance. Three more for Engineering were jammed into the south-east quadrant. Physics moved out of the old Natural Philosophy Building near the centre of the campus to a purpose-built facility at the top-end

Described by a professor of architecture as the university's most impressive interior space, the South Car Park has been used by students for balls and by film-makers for its atmospheric effect. (Property and Buildings)

of Swanston Street. Geology moved across the road to a building on the corner of Swanston and Elgin Streets, linked to the main campus by a pedestrian bridge.

Some of these additions were forbidding exercises in concrete, others created canyons of brick. The most severe was the Arts Centre of the Teachers' College on the corner of Swanston and Grattan Streets, hard up against the ornate splendour of the original building. The most genteel was the Council Chamber built in 1970 to finally close the south side of the Quadrangle. It was faced with the same stone as the original wings, and its supporting columns mimicked the cloisters. A similar nostalgia was apparent in the habit of attaching the prefix 'Old' to the original purpose of an edifice: hence Old Arts, Old Commerce, Old Geology, Old Physics and even Old Pathology.

The John Medley Building seen under construction from the cloisters of the Quadrangle. The war memorial in the middle ground would be moved when construction of the underground car park began.

Public spaces were planted with native species to soften the hard edges of an overbuilt campus, as in this area between Old Arts and the Baillieu Library. (courtesy Rick de Carteret)

The cumulative effect of decades of haphazard growth reduced lawns to mud trails that were then sealed with bitumen. As Carrick Chambers, professor of Botany and subsequent chairman of the grounds committee put it, 'the ground space between buildings was shrinking and much of what was left of a once-great landscape had fallen into decay'. From the ruins of its former park setting, the university's Master Planner, Bryce Mortlock, created a pedestrian network of linked and landscaped courts, paved or flagged, and planted with native species to integrate the buildings with the open spaces. One measure of his success was the return of bird life. There was even some conservation, the Old Physics Building spared from demolition and used as a gallery for the university's substantial art collection.

The time of troubles passed with the dismissal of the Whitlam government at the end of 1975, and the pace of change slowed. Student protest
proved ineffectual when the School of Business Administration's proposal to
establish a residential centre, condemned by *Farrago* as a 'business man's
motel' and resisted by the Assembly, was endorsed by the Council in that year.
Student power was weakened further in 1977 when a member of the Liberal
Club challenged compulsory membership of the Students Representative
Council and the use of its fees for political activities. While his legal action
ultimately failed, Liberal ministers of education at the state and federal level
curbed student unions.

Small groups of student activists pursued these and other internecine disputes as an increasingly arcane activity of decreasing interest to the student
body. The changed mood was evident in the colleges, which had struggled to
fill their residential places when students preferred the freedom of communal
living. Most colleges had gone co-residential and relaxed their supervision.
Now they were back in favour as places of boisterous indulgence for the
jeunesse dorée. Yet study had become more unremitting now that continuous
assessment—another legacy of educational reform—had replaced the distant
end-of-year exam.

The change of federal government brought an end to the era of rapid
expansion. The number of students in Australian universities had increased
threefold in the previous decade, and the number of universities from twelve
to eighteen; just one additional university followed over the next ten years
and student numbers grew by barely 20 per cent. Melbourne, which had
stabilised its enrolment at around 14 000 students, coped more easily with the
circumscription than newer universities such as La Trobe and Deakin. But
Melbourne shared the financial rigours of a progressive reduction in funding
per student as the Fraser government bore down on public expenditure. With
no other means of increasing the university's resources, David Derham's
warning of dependence on the Commonwealth was quickly realised.

The universities felt this parsimony as a punitive measure for their progressive sympathies, and reasserted the contribution they made as public
institutions to the national welfare. It took some time for them to appreciate

that the ground had shifted. The economy no longer responded to the government's levers and no longer provided the regular increases of revenue that had allowed the expansion of the public sector since the Second World War. Nor did it absorb the ready entry of graduates into the workforce. A falling birth-rate, cuts in immigration and a levelling off in school completion rates removed the dynamic that had propelled public education for the past three decades.

The government contemplated the reintroduction of fees for second degrees in 1976 and again in 1981, when the threat revived mass student protest and scuttled the proposal. Australia thus retained the arrangements that had been built up during the post-war boom—university places for all qualified to study, free of charge, and provided from the public purse through national allocation—even though a crucial condition of those arrangements no longer operated. The government would not meet their cost. For the next decade policy remained frozen.

That did not mean an absence of government activity. On the contrary, the policy deadlock produced a host of interventions. The Fraser government created a Tertiary Education Commission in 1977 to bring the universities, the colleges of advanced education and the technical and further education colleges under common co-ordination. The binary divide remained, and the Commonwealth encouraged the growth of technical and further education, which cost much less and was largely funded by the States. The Victorian government, for its part, created a Post-Secondary Education Commission that claimed authority over the entire sector, including the universities with which it had severed all financial links. The Staff Association, meanwhile, was shaking off the inhibitions of a professional body as the membership turned to industrial bargaining. After the national organisation obtained registration, wages and conditions were determined by the Arbitration Commission.

As if this were not enough, the school sector and the teachers unions were contesting the authority of the Victorian universities over the curriculum and assessment of the Higher School Certificate. They wanted to free it from the tyranny of university selection in the interests of pupils whose inclinations lay elsewhere. Indeed, many school-leavers were choosing to enrol at colleges in preference to the newer universities. Demand for places at Melbourne remained strong, though Derham characteristically insisted that this remain confidential.

It became common during the late 1970s to refer to the universities as in a 'steady state', but those charged with the task of management were kept constantly busy. The Commonwealth expected them to do more with less. Its reduction of funding (from $2300 per student in 1975 to $2182 in 1982), along with the increase in salaries as younger staff were promoted, meant larger classes and heavier workloads. The curtailment of capital grants and research funding made for shortages of equipment and cuts in library acquisition. Melbourne's improved budgetary management allowed for economies to be absorbed without severe damage to its teaching and research. Some of the changes in this period were probably beneficial: the abolition of separate honours streams in lower years improved the quality of undergraduate education; the separation of large, compulsory subjects into optional units made for greater flexibility and more inter-disciplinary studies. One legacy of the student discontent had been much greater attention to pedagogy, teaching support and educational technology. There were fewer notoriously poor lecturers and progression rates had improved.

The research performance was patchy. Medicine, science, engineering and agricultural science did best in the increasingly competitive climate, though even they had weak as well as strong areas. Growth of the biological sciences was inexorable, spearheaded by the consistent success of the Medical Faculty in obtaining grants for its impressive research program, so that its 'research only' staff already outnumbered those who combined teaching and research. The faculty's access to a separate funding body, the National Health and Medical Research Council, was a decided advantage, while the neighbouring Walter and Eliza Hall Institute and the Florey Institute, had attained world standing.

Other professional faculties took longer to adapt to the grant system and depended on the university's distribution of Commonwealth funds for their scholarships and research projects. The creation of a new Joint Committee for

Research and Graduate Studies, and the appointment in 1975 of John Poynter as Deputy Vice-Chancellor with responsibility for research, signalled that this eleemosynary arrangement was on notice. When the Commonwealth finally began to direct more of its funds to outstanding groups of researchers, Melbourne won two of the first round of Special Research Centres in 1982—one for Cancer and Transplantation led by Ian McKenzie at the Austin Hospital, and the other in Plant Cell Biology led by Bruce Knox and Adrienne Clarke, who was promoted to a personal chair in 1985.

One consequence of the financial dependence upon government was a decline in private support. The Miegunyah bequest, realised in 1973 and providing generous support to Melbourne University Press, the Library and the university's art collection as well as Biochemistry, had been arranged before the death of Russell Grimwade nearly twenty years earlier. Chairs were now endowed by companies with a direct interest in the activity of their incumbents. Melbourne businessmen raised large sums when the Fraser government offered to establish the Graduate School of Management in 1982, but on condition that it was detached from the Faculty of Economics and Commerce and given its own board and its own premises south of Grattan Street. A measure of the independence of the Melbourne Business School (as it became) was the separation of its library from that of the university, so that students are still astonished to discover that they cannot borrow items it holds as its own. The ties that Priestley had devised to bind the university to its community had fallen into decrepitude, and it was Davis McCaughey, as Deputy Chancellor, who sought to revive them in 1984 with the creation of an Alumni Association. Its potential has still to be realised.

McCaughey's period of office ended in 1986 when he became Governor of Victoria. His predecessor, Sir Ninian Stephen, was lost to Yarralumla in 1982. The Deputy's role was well served; that of the Chancellor remained contentious. Sir Charles Lowe had been succeeded in 1954 by another judge of the Supreme Court, Sir Arthur Dean, whose preference for *in camera* proceedings served the university ill as public criticism mounted. He was followed briefly by Sir William Upjohn, a surgeon, who made way in 1967 for Sir Robert Menzies. Much was expected of Melbourne's most illustrious

Adrienne Clarke was appointed to a personal chair in biology in 1985, and subsequently chaired CSIRO and served as Lieutenant-Governor of Victoria. (Media and Publications)

Sir Robert Menzies, inducted as Chancellor in 1967, takes up his duty flanked by the outgoing Vice-Chancellor, Sir George Paton. (*University of Melbourne Gazette,* May 1967)

graduate and the greatest public benefactor of the Australian universities. Having observed the damage an over-active chancellor could do, Menzies provided staunch support for Derham during the student protests while facilitating some of the necessary compromises. If he had not been so disdainful of the radicals, he might have helped avoid the confrontations that forced these belated concessions, but his powers were failing even before a stroke forced resignation in 1972.

◊ ◊ ◊

The election of Leonard Weickhardt, research director of ICI, marked a break from the dynasty of legal and medical knights, and suggested that the reformers had gained the upper hand. But in a contested election Weickhardt was succeeded in 1978 by yet another Supreme Court judge, Sir Oliver Gillard. The pugnacious Pansy Wright, who in retirement was senior Deputy Chancellor, had expected to win and blamed Sir David Derham (knighted in 1977) and Sir Lance Townsend, the Dean of Medicine and a bitter foe, for his defeat. He might have attributed the loss to his commoner status; instead, he suggested that the freemasons were responsible. Gillard collapsed following his first Council meeting in the chair, and Wright donned the Chancellor's robes in 1980.

The new Chancellor was instinctively suspicious of executive authority and a persistent critic of 'the administration', an increasingly common epithet bundling together both the external and internal pressures that were reducing academic autonomy. Wright had previously used the Academic Board and later the Council to cross-examine the Vice-Chancellor and his officers. He now exercised his right *ex officio* to attend all manner of university committees and demand answers to his inquiries. Derham suffered such interference with difficulty. His health was failing and he retired early in 1982.

Wright then exercised an extraordinary chancellorial licence. Without even advertising the vacancy, he invited David Caro, the former professor of Physics and Deputy Vice-Chancellor from 1972 to 1977, to become the new Vice-Chancellor, and secured his appointment. Colin Howard, professor of

Roy Douglas Wright, universally known as 'Pansy', perambulates his domain after election to the office of Chancellor in 1980. The robes were more precious to him than his demeanour suggests. (Media and Publications)

David Caro addresses a reunion of alumni in London in 1983. A man of singular courtesy, he affirmed the scholarly mission.

Law and Chair of the Academic Board, called a special meeting of the Board to protest against this summary procedure. David Penington, the new Dean of Medicine, joined in the criticism.

With law and medicine linked in opposition to the manner of his appointment, Caro's position was unenviable. Like Derham, he had interrupted distinguished service at Melbourne for several years—in his case as Vice-Chancellor of the University of Tasmania—before he took up the reins. Courteous and diplomatic, Caro's authority derived from a lucid intellect. He was not a driving vice-chancellor and disdained the self-promotion that was an increasing characteristic of those rising to leadership in the country's universities. His Registrar, Jim Potter, had moved across in 1979 from a senior academic post in the Department of Electrical Engineering, and might have been expected to bridge the divide that Wright and others resented. He brought a brisk efficiency that made the poachers feel one of their own had turned gamekeeper.

The new team was quickly faced with additional demands from the university's niggardly paymasters. The election of a Labor government in 1983 brought sweeping economic reform but precious little relief to the university sector. There was a recognition that Australia had fallen behind in the new international economy, an appreciation that a well-educated workforce was crucial to its future prosperity, and an awareness that the gap between research and industry had to be closed. There was also a determination not to repeat Whitlam's venture into open-ended public provision. The Labor Party's earlier pursuit of social justice through comprehensive arrangements gave way to equity programs 'targeted'—a telling word—to those disadvantaged by gender, ethnicity or disability, though seldom class. At the same time visa charges for international students, first introduced in 1980, were increased, and a limit imposed of 10 per cent of all enrolments.

The restriction on international students was a makeshift response to a shortage of places. With no resolution of the contradiction inherent in free, public universities that were denied the funds needed to meet a growing demand, the pressures could only build. Melbourne once more examined its activities, ended some moribund courses, and merged a few departments. In 1984 Caro abandoned the budget formula he had devised, so that funds were allocated to faculties on a historical basis, with modifications that he could control. This afforded some much-needed relief to the Library, and preserved research funding. Such were the limits of the steady-state university.

◊ ◊ ◊

Then came a change in Canberra, and the pent-up force for change was released. In 1987 John Dawkins, one of the government's most impatient reformers, became the Minister of an expanded Department of Employment, Education and Training (DEET). The conjunction was ominous. He quickly abolished the Tertiary Education Commission, thereby removing its university members and other academic interest groups from influence over policy. In their place Dawkins brought a group of like-minded higher education officers together in an informal 'Purple Circle'; they included the new Vice-Chancellor of Monash, Mal Logan, but no one from the university establishment with which Melbourne was familiar. Dawkins seized and kept the initiative, brushing aside all objections. At the end of the year he released a blueprint for a radical restructure. It was called *Higher Education: a policy discussion paper* and was followed eight months later by *Higher Education: a policy statement*. The difference between the first, 'green' paper and the final white one was scarcely discernible.

Dawkins abolished the distinction between universities and other tertiary institutions in favour of a Unified National System. By laying down minimum sizes for Commonwealth funding, he set off a wave of mergers over the next few years that reworked the country's 19 universities and 46 colleges of advanced education into 36 universities, some of them with substantial TAFE (Technical and Further Education) components. It was a Unified National System in which all participants were funded on a similar basis, and required to furnish enormous volumes of standardised data to demonstrate their compliance with government policy on staffing, credit transfer, a common academic year and much else. They were expected to streamline their government, professionalise their management, formulate strategic plans, reduce cumbersome collegial procedures, strengthen the hand of the 'chief executive officer'.

The wave of mergers in any case fostered this restructuring of internal organisation, throwing up new layers of corporate managers across far-flung campuses. Universities such as Monash and Sydney grasped the opportunity for expansion. Melbourne was more cautious and took in just three institutions, the neighbouring Melbourne College of Advanced Education, the smaller Hawthorn College of Advanced Education and the dispersed Victorian College of Agriculture and Horticulture. (It also assisted the fledgling

University of Ballarat through a temporary affiliation agreement, and later formed a similar partnership with the Victorian College of the Arts, which became an affiliated institution while continuing to operate under its own statute.) An enrolment of 14 574 EFTSU (a new acronym for the basic unit of currency, an equivalent full-time student) in 1988 thus increased to 24 060 by 1992.

Dawkins encouraged an expansion of the Unified National System, which increased from 394 000 enrolments in the year he took charge to 634 000 in the last year of the Labor government. Given the fiscal constraint, Dawkins' Green Paper had insisted that part of the cost would have to come from the non-government sector, and in 1989 he reintroduced fees for domestic students, with a deferred payment scheme, set on average at 20 per cent of the cost of the course. Full fees could be charged for international students and subsequently for vocational postgraduate courses. While reducing its proportional contribution, the Commonwealth increased control. In their annual negotiations with the Department, universities had to gain approval of their teaching 'profile', and from 1990 the Commonwealth allocated funds for teaching according to a relative funding model.

The Unified National System broke the nexus between teaching and research. The Commonwealth sequestered part of its operating grants to the universities for distribution on a competitive basis by an Australian Research Council (ARC). Since the success rate of applicants was one in five, many academics were deprived of research support. Universities had previously allowed considerable latitude to different modes of scholarship. The procedures of the ARC imposed a common model of scientist discovery. It shifted the balance from pure research to what it called 'strategic basic research' with defined outcomes and applications to 'national economic and social problems'.

Some feared that research would become a residual activity. It retained its status, both for individual academics and institutions, but became a source of increasing anxiety for both. The former colleges embarked on a strenuous effort to compete with the older universities, often to the detriment of their established mission. The older universities were distracted by the tasks of digesting what they had swallowed, while pursuing the new opportunities for fee income. The chief casualties of the large, comprehensive university were intimacy and diversity.

This was the revolution that Dawkins set in train, and Melbourne was ill-placed to resist it. An old, exclusive and cumbersome university jealous of its autonomy, it represented the *ancien regime* that the Minister held in contempt. Insofar as it compared itself with others, it aspired to recognition as a university of world standing and found the levelling tendencies of the Unified National System deeply disturbing. Used to exercising influence in closed circles, it was locked out of the 'Purple Circle' and grew accustomed to discovery that a purposeful Mal Logan of Monash was a step or two ahead. Upon the retirement of David Caro at the end of 1987, Melbourne turned to a new Vice-Chancellor with a mission.

◊ ◊ ◊

David Penington was to all outward appearances a pillar of the Melbourne establishment. Educated, like Paton and Derham, at Scotch College, he had studied medicine at Melbourne and Oxford and practised in Harley Street before taking up a chair in the Medical Faculty. The pedigree was deceptive. Penington had been a moderniser in the hospitals, a pioneer of community medicine in the Whitlam era, a reforming Dean, an adviser on health policy to the Cain Labor government, and a courageous leader of the national AIDS taskforce. Throughout his advancement he demonstrated a capacity for forming judgements and holding to them that was unusual in a hierarchical institution where most learned how to bow to a superior force. Now he was in command, and no one ever doubted it.

Penington's advent brought a policy statement, 'Planning for Change', and much change followed. Some of it was structural: a thorough overhaul of the university's committee system that strengthened the hand of those charged with the implementation of the university's plans. Some was organisational: the incorporation of the activities of the Melbourne College, chiefly into the Faculty of Education; the absorption of Dentistry, the inclusion of

David Penington at the lectern. As the chief
opponent of John Dawkins' procrustean
Unified National System, he relished such
opportunities. (Media and Publications)

physiotherapy and postgraduate nursing, and the transfer of psychology into
the Faculty of Medicine, Dentistry and Health Sciences. Corresponding
changes to the student organisations saw the amalgamation of the Students
Representative Council, the Student Union and the union of the Melbourne
College into Melbourne University Student Union Incorporated. That suffix,
so antithetical to the spirit of an earlier generation of student radicals, indicated its commercialisation of service provision. The growing range of fran-
chised outlets and boutique food-counters turned the Union House into a
new kind of shop, a retail mall.

The larger change was procedural: most notably, the introduction of a
system of annual appraisal of all staff as part of a management system where
the lines of authority were clear. Penington saw this clarification of responsibilities as lifting the burden of administrative regulation from academics.

Sir Edward Woodward, Chancellor from 1990 to 2001, brought a warmth and dignity to degree conferrals. Here he presents Nancy Millis—who became Chancellor of La Trobe University after retiring from a chair in microbiology—with an honorary doctorate of science. (Media and Publications)

He preferred academic officers to administrative ones. The Vice-Principal retired and a trio of new Deputy Vice-Chancellors was appointed, with clear portfolios. Barry Sheehan, the former director of the Melbourne College, took charge of resources in 1989; Frank Larkins, who had been Professor of Chemistry at the University of Tasmania, assumed responsibility for research in 1990; and Boris Schedvin, Professor of Economic History, handled academic issues from 1991. Penington drove them hard and himself harder.

The new broom swept clean. Caro had tolerated the diminished activity of the University Assembly; Penington abolished it. The Chancellor, who voiced his misgivings with the new regime, was faced with a new provision for triennial re-election, tested support and announced his resignation at the end of 1989. His successor was Sir Edward Woodward, a Federal Court judge, who maintained the authority of the chancellor's office by exercising it more judiciously.

David Penington was as insistent a reformer as John Dawkins, the agent of change whom he so frequently challenged. He saw the new regimen of the Unified National System as a threat to university autonomy and inimical to the values that the University of Melbourne nurtured. Where others shrank from confrontation, Penington waged a public campaign against constant intrusions by the Department of Employment, Education and Training. He denounced the redistribution of resources, the 'claw-backs' and the funding formulae that pressed his university onto the Procrustean bed of the Unified National System. He took particular issue with the instrumental approach to education implicit in its association with employment and training, and the associated codification of a national system of skills and competencies. This spilled over into his campaign against the state government's new Victorian Certificate of Education, which he saw as an inappropriate preparation for tertiary study, and he forced change. The bonus points he won for mathematics and languages other than English have saved those subjects from their fate in other school systems: three times as many Victorians study foreign languages in year twelve as their counterparts in New South Wales. Within the university the ailing language departments were revived in 1992 with the formation of an enhanced School of Languages.

In all this Penington was an outspoken champion of the university, but he appreciated that it was acutely vulnerable. Dawkins had begun his political career in the National Union of Australian University Students during the early 1970s, and his memories of slipshod teaching and unresponsive university administrators were shared by many of his colleagues in the parliament and the public service. Universities had to set their house in order if they were to ward off the accusations of inefficiency and self-serving academic practices.

The Academic Board, composed of the university's professors and heads of department, serves as its parliament. Portraits of former Chancellors look down from the walls. David Penington sits to the right of the president in 1990, Graeme Ryan. (courtesy Rick de Carteret)

This was the message that Penington drove home in university forums. His lengthy addresses to the Academic Board dominated its proceedings. He supplemented them in conferences of heads at rural retreats, reiterated them with messages to staff in the university's internal newsletter. It was a highly personal style, most effective in more intimate settings: more than one professor resigned after the Vice-Chancellor discussed his future plans for improvement. When problems became apparent in particular departments or faculties, heads rolled. Long-overdue departures made it possible to fill chairs with young and talented professors who began to transform the work of their departments.

The emphasis was on improvement of teaching and research through measures that would ensure its quality was demonstrable. Melbourne took advantage of the new opportunities for specialist postgraduate courses, and expanded its postgraduate research numbers: doctoral candidates increased from less than 1000 in 1990 to nearly 1800 in 1995. The original '1888' building of the Melbourne College was turned into a Graduate Centre, housing a School of Graduate Studies with its own Dean and a newly invigorated postgraduate association, all providing a wide range of support services for the postgraduate body. Melbourne did not set out to recruit large numbers of international students, as other universities did in the early 1990s, nor did it venture into foreign partnerships and offshore campuses. Its strategy was to secure international standing through the excellence of its research, and the effort saw Melbourne regain primacy in the competition for grants from the Australian Research Council and the National Health and Medical Research Council.

These achievements were trumpeted in annual reports and ancillary publications that became increasingly glossy, for such was the currency of exchange in the universities as they were drawn into competition for market share. No promotional literature was complete without photographs of a beaming achiever and an accompanying puff-piece from a publicist unconcerned by the difference between a transitive and an intransitive verb. Some longed to read the headline 'University does middling well'.

Still, Melbourne withstood the challenges of the Unified National System and Penington saw out Dawkins, who moved on to the Treasury in 1991 and retired from parliament shortly after the 1993 election. In that election Penington was identified as a member of the 'kitchen cabinet' of the Liberal leader; but Labor was returned and the Vice-Chancellor completed his term at the end of 1995. In defending the university he had transformed it, putting it onto a war footing in which the chain of command prevailed. He ruled by a command of detail and strategy. No one surpassed his knowledge of the minutiae of administration. No one who sought an audience was turned away. Email responses to queries—Penington came late to the digital revolution but he ensured the university had a fibre optic network by 1991—

came at impossibly early hours of the day. They were brisk and direct; he was incapable of dissimulation. With this went a forensic grasp of the university's organisational logic and a genuine commitment to its academic values. It was a powerful combination, so powerful that it was difficult to shake his conviction once it was formed. He beat down challenges and reacted angrily to his own misjudgements. Stern moralism was his shield and his sword.

◊ ◊ ◊

David Penington took a keen interest in the choice of his successor, and it was therefore all the more surprising that Alan Gilbert should be so different. He was the first Vice-Chancellor since 1938 to assume the post with no previous Melbourne connection—for nearly half a century the university had drawn its leaders from the city's two leading private schools; now it had an outsider. Gilbert was a historian, who had studied at the Australian National University and then taught briefly at the fledgling University of Papua New Guinea. After further study at Oxford, he rose through the ranks at the University of New South Wales and served a five-year spell as Vice-Chancellor in Tasmania. To a strongly traditional and hierarchical university still catching its breath after Peningon's driving program of improvement, Gilbert brought the management style of Kensington, NSW: less personal, more systematic.

Faced with a problem, Penington's instinct was to impose an appropriate solution. Gilbert was more interested in the articulation of strategies that would free the university from the need for expedient remedies. A student of the past, he prophesied dramatic change in the knowledge economy. A scholar with an appreciation of genuine scholarship and unusual eloquence in his celebration of it, he had read his way through the curriculum of the business school and mastered the language of the corporate world. He seldom personalised issues and was unusually open to argument, though less available for it than Penington. Gilbert seemed at times to float above the concerns that weighed down his colleagues, for his attention was fixed on the strategic horizon.

Alan Gilbert takes stock. This Vice-Chancellor's capacity for advocacy, often audacious but always closely reasoned, is one of his strengths. Erudite allusions come with PowerPoint presentations of data; his left hand might even be resting on the keyboard. (Media and Publications)

'The Melbourne Agenda' embodied his strategic vision for the university: that it should become a world-class international university. To do this, it must free itself from the constraints of Australian higher education, which was falling further behind leading overseas universities in its resources and performance. Gilbert thought that Australia could sustain no more than two or three universities of this standing, and saw little chance that government would provide the level of support they needed, a proposition he demonstrated in PowerPoint presentations that compared Melbourne's resources with those of comparable North American universities. Some of his statements suggested a preference for private funding because of the greater independence it would afford. This had been implicit in Derham's warnings, and was in keeping with the shrinkage of public purpose and capacity, though

Gilbert's outspoken advocacy of greater differentiation of the country's universities antagonised those who worked in the more straitened ones. In any case he saw national benefit in Melbourne lifting itself out of the ruck. Less often noticed was his commitment to the maintenance of strong faculties of Arts and science at a time when other vice-chancellors were allowing theirs to wither.

To this end he embarked on a series of linked initiatives. The first was an ambitious scholarship program designed to attract the best undergraduate students from across the country. By 1997, when the first scholarships were awarded, there was sufficient differentiation within the Unified National System for interstate movement to have begun, and Melbourne was able to enrol outstanding school-leavers from other states. But the program attracted little external funding and, once other universities responded with their own scholarships, the bidding war depleted resources.

Scholarship assistance fed into the second initiative, which was to attract fee-paying students. The Coalition government that took office in 1996 confirmed a decision of the previous Labor government not to supplement universities for increases in staff salaries. Instead, it allowed them to offer up to a quarter of the number of funded places in all undergraduate courses except medicine to Australian students on a fee-paying basis. Some universities rejected the invitation on grounds of a principled commitment to merit-based public education; others recognised that they would attract few customers. Melbourne's prestige was such that it could offer such places without reducing the entry level below the floor for those admitted on the usual basis, and scholarships for able or necessitous students increased the flow. There were over a thousand of them by 2002, more than in any other university, and they were spread across all the faculties.

The third departure was to recruit international students. Melbourne had previously held aloof from this market, whose rapid growth after earlier restrictions were lifted confirmed the Vice-Chancellor's prediction of a growing world demand for tertiary education. It had refrained in the knowledge that Australian universities operated as a cheap alternative provider for those unable to gain entry to the United States or the United Kingdom, with consequences for their quality and reputation. Once Melbourne entered the market as a price-leader with commensurate academic standards, it made swift progress. International enrolments increased from less than 2000 in 1996 to over 6500 by 2002.

International recruitment augmented the university's fee income—which reached $170 million by 2003, fast approaching the Commonwealth's teaching grant of $200 million—and kept it solvent. Accompanying the arrival of these students from overseas was a further innovation, the formation of an international network of universities that Gilbert named Universitas 21. This was one of the Vice-Chancellor's personal schemes, and he spent much time forming and shaping it. It linked three Australian universities (Melbourne, New South Wales and Queensland) to similar, comprehensive and research-intensive universities, twelve initially, in New Zealand, South-East Asia, North America and the United Kingdom (there are now further European and Chinese members). While the formation of Universitas 21 caused some domestic chagrin, the purpose, other than co-operation, exchange and prestigious association, was less clear. It soon took shape in an agreement with Thomsons Corporation to form a global online university. Here again Gilbert played the leading role and Melbourne took a larger financial stake in Universitas Global than any of the other participants in Universitas 21.

Gilbert sought a similar partnership with the private sector through the formation in 1997 of Melbourne University Private. Other Australian universities had created commercial agencies to conduct business with the private sector; this was to be a full degree-granting body, which would draw on university staff to provide courses tailored to corporate needs and free of the restrictions that the Commonwealth imposed on the public universities. Melbourne University Private was meant to attract substantial corporate investment and build a large volume of business. It was to move into new purpose-built accommodation south of Grattan Street. Adding 50 000 square metres to the academic space, the University Square project was by far the largest and boldest of its building programs. It required the removal of a bowling club on Crown land, the demolition of several terrace houses and a

New and old: a view of University Square from Grattan Street. The Melbourne Business School defines the eastern perimeter (left) and the Law School forms the southern one. The bulk of the new office blocks contrasts with the historic terrace houses, while the roughly textured walls of the car park entrances and plant rooms that rise out of the plaza (foreground) adjoin an alley of trees on the old square. (Media and Publications)

large loan for the construction of three bulky edifices of corporate design and a five-level underground carpark. Upon its completion as the university marked one hundred and fifty years, University Square broke the constraints on the campus, allowed the removal of unsightly annexes from the Quad-rangle at its historic centre, opened up its southern precinct and shifted activity from the service facilities on the northern perimeter.

But before University Square was completed it was apparent that Melbourne University Private would be only a minor tenant. It attracted just one business partner, found fewer clients than expected—and most of them preferred that the educational services be brought to them rather than delivered in South Carlton. After reporting losses, the capital base was expanded by merging Melbourne Enterprises International (MEI) into Melbourne University Private. MEI had been formed out of the extremely enterprising business unit of the former Hawthorn College. It was a beneficiary, when Melbourne IT was floated on the stock exchange late in 1999, of an operation that sold Internet domain names, an activity begun with amateur enthusiasm by a technical officer in the Engineering Faculty long before its commercial implications were apparent. Melbourne IT attracted investors who pushed the shares far above the issue price. The university incurred criticism both for undervaluing the shares and for allowing the underwriters to allocate some to members of the Council. The first of these criticisms abated as the flurry abated and the shares fell below par. Most of the proceeds went to university projects and some to MEI as it sought to revive the fortunes of Melbourne University Private.

The University was therefore left with two large, debt-financed buildings, for which fortunately it had abundant demand. The rapid growth of international students (6500 by 2002) was matched by the increase in fee-paying domestic students in postgraduate as well as undergraduate courses (another 3300), more postgraduate research candidates (2900) and more research staff (830) with their insistence on greater space, better technology and improved facilities. The construction of the Ian Potter Museum of Art on Swanston Street provided a stylish facility for the university's art collection. A similar use of steel and glass for the Sidney Myer Asia Centre to its south emphasised the difference in standard with the adjoining Alice Hoy Building, a relic of the post-war style of public works.

The life-cycle of buildings was shrinking. Those built in the 1970s rapidly succumbed to 'Ding' Dyason's toilet test of obsolescence as females outnumbered males in almost every faculty. The gender profile was a broad base with a narrow peak. Female undergraduates flowed into postgraduate study and then into academic careers, only to find the upper levels remained obdurately masculine. There was a greater preponderance of women among the administrative staff, but men headed most of the divisions. Melbourne did

If the English acquired an empire in a fit of absence of mind, the university built up a remarkable collection of works of art by both inadvertence and foresight. The Ian Potter Museum of Art was made possible by generous benefactions, and allows for its conservation and exhibition. (Media and Publications)

Fay Marles joined the Council as State Commissioner for Equal Opportunity, and brought to the university a concern for social justice. In 2001 she became Chancellor. (Media and Publications) better than most Australian universities, but the imbalance at the top was visible at the Academic Board, where men embraced the role of Head of Department, and at degree ceremonies, where male deans read out the names of graduands. Female leadership programs helped women to overcome these disadvantages. The installation of Fay Marles as Chancellor in 2001, and the appointment of Sally Walker as Senior Deputy Vice-Chancellor strengthened efforts to do better.

Departmental headship had become an increasingly onerous responsibility as the tasks of management expanded. Gilbert followed Penington in the move to line management, bringing the formulation of policy and the allocation of resources together in a Planning and Budget Committee, which consisted of the senior administrators and the deans. He respected the authority of the Academic Board, which retained responsibility for academic standards, so that managers had to conform to its policies while they met the university's goals. Gilbert's maxim was plan-driven, incentive-based budgeting, which was expressed in a formula (modifying the funding formula of the Commonwealth) that allocated funds to faculties with rewards and penalties for meeting the university's objectives. The faculties in turn created their own sticks and carrots as they passed these funds, along with those they earned through their recruitment of fee students and their research and consultancy activity, on to their departments. It was an odd budgetary system for a university that aspired to break out of Australian mediocrity into the status of a world-class university.

◊ ◊ ◊

As if to affirm the resilience of the academic endeavour, the constitution of these faculties and departments displayed a remarkable continuity. As other Australian universities reformed into divisions, merged faculties and conglomerate schools, Melbourne's stability was all the more distinctive. If we compare the present organisational structure with the one that Derham had inherited, the persistence of disciplines is striking. The largest faculties, then and now, are Arts, medicine and science.

The Faculty of Arts lost some departments (such as Indian Studies), while its other language departments were reformed in the 1990s into the School of Languages and the Melbourne Institute of Asian Languages and Societies. It absorbed Creative Arts, Criminology and Social Work, and spawned new programmes such as Aboriginal studies, anthropology, cinema studies, cultural studies, media and communication, social theory and sociology. Longstanding arguments between the ancients and the moderns were exacerbated by the zeal of the postmoderns, yet English, history and political science remain the largest departments. The faculty had 6114 equivalent full-time students in 2002; it earned one-twentieth of the research income, and produced more than a fifth of the research publications.

Medicine, Dentistry and Health Sciences expanded to take in Dentistry, postgraduate Nursing, Physiotherapy and Psychology. It developed a large School of Population Health as emphasis on the social and cultural dimensions of health increased, and maintained its clinical teaching throughout drastic changes to the hospital system. The intensification of the biological sciences is apparent in the mutation of key departments: Anatomy *and Cell Biology*, Biochemistry *and Molecular Biology*, Microbiology *and Immunology*. The faculty has 5398 students, and accounts for half the university's income from national competitive grants. The Cochlear implant hearing device developed by Graeme Clark as Professor of Otolaryngology and the recruitment of the Nobel prizewinning immunologist Peter Doherty are indicators of its outstanding research performance.

Science underwent even less organisational change. Botany, Chemistry, Genetics, Physics and Zoology continue. Mathematics merged with Statistics, Geology buckled into Earth Sciences, a Department of Computation generated Information Science and then Information Systems. The rapid growth of the high-tech sector brought science and industry closer than ever, but created strains for a general faculty. Science contributes to other professional faculties and provides the knowledge base for new fields, but finds its core disciplines under strain. The faculty has 4198 students and is second only to medicine in research grants.

Engineering also kept some of its core departments, such as Chemical Engineering, and enlarged others. Hence Civil *and Environmental* Engineering; Electrical *and Electronic* Engineering; Mechanical *and Manufacturing* Engineering. Mining and Surveying yielded to Geomatics, and the growth of information technology produced a large Department of Computer Science and Software Engineering. Strong international recruitment contributed to the faculty's 2967 students.

The former Faculty of Agriculture, meanwhile, took in Forestry and then the College of Agriculture and Horticulture to form an Institute of Land and Food Resources. Its challenge was to adapt activities to the changing circumstances of agribusiness, for as family farms dwindled, parents no longer sent their children to the rural agricultural colleges. After changes to staffing and curriculum, the Institute has 970 students in degree courses.

Education experienced a similar growth as it absorbed the bulk of the former Melbourne College, and a similar contraction as demand for schoolteachers declined. After a shift to graduate training and a growing emphasis on education policy and management, there are now four departments and 2818 students. The vigorous Centre for the Study of Higher Education contributed to higher education policy and improvement of the university's teaching.

Veterinary Science, on the other hand, remained small and extremely attractive to its 366 students. It is more research-intensive—the cost of this discipline constrains it. Other smaller faculties felt the same pinch on their capacity. Architecture and Building took in the previously free-standing Department of Town and Regional Planning, but the architecture profession remained its principal point of reference and intervened during the 1980s to secure improvements. The faculty then embarked on impressive recruitment and now has 1246 students, who have exhausted its studio space. Music has to send its 535 students to all points of the compass for their instrumental practice.

The Faculty of Law was more fortunate. Along with Medicine, it serves the university's most prestigious profession and takes its pick of school-

The University's arms are based on a seal designed by the artist, Ludwig Becker, in 1855. It showed a winged female figure holding a wreath of laurel. She is Nike, a Greek goddess of Victory. The name (Victoria in Latin) alludes to the newly separated colony, and the stars of the Southern Cross that appear on the State's arms. The University motto, *Postera Crescam Laude*, embellishes the same theme. The University obtained a Grant of Arms from the College of Heralds in 1863. It shows a Victory soberly clad and posed calmly between four stars.

The university commissioned a new design for its Jubilee in 1906, based on an elegant Nike in a Constantinople museum; with one knee raised, she is in flight.

Variations appear in the Vice Chancellor's residence and in the former Moot Court (left). Douglas Annand took further liberties for the emblem he designed for Melbourne University Press in 1947 (right).

In 1991 the university embarked on an Image Project that was intended to show a more energetic Victory and create 'a stronger, more professional' image. Strangely, the public relations firm that undertook the project suggested the arms be stripped of their Victorian characteristics. The 1992 design overlaid the arms with an enlarged scroll to make the motto more visible, extended Victory's wings outside the shield, and added a fifth star to make up the Southern Cross.

leavers for the undergraduate component of its 1745 students. While under-graduate teaching broadened from the mastery of black-letter law to a more analytical and international curriculum, the faculty was quick to grasp the opportunity of fee-paying postgraduate coursework in specialist fields. It resisted fragmentation into departments and instead created a range of centres for staff to pursue their particular interests. From the symbolic centre of the university it moved in 2002 to the grandest of the University Square buildings.

Economics and Commerce, with 4194 students, was the greatest benefici-ary of international recruitment and paid careful attention to consumer demand. Economists exerted unprecedented influence in the closing decades of the twentieth century. Like mathematics, economics became a master-discipline, and again like mathematics it took on a crystalline purity of abstraction. Accordingly, Economic Geography and Economic History dis-appeared, while Legal Studies became Business Law and then was dis-patched to the Faculty of Law. Yet even the economists felt the pinch of commercial competition from Management and Financial Studies, while Accounting expanded into Business Information Systems.

This rapid survey suggests the durability of the university's organisation as well as the adaptability of its components. Internal competition encourages mercantilist habits; mutual interest fosters co-operation. A common points system and a centralised timetable allowed a growing number of students to pursue joint degrees. A number of the faculties created an Office for Environmental Programs to co-ordinate the teaching of a popular masters course. Many of them shared in the planning of a new Molecular Science and Biotechnology Institute as part of *Bio 21*, a co-operative venture of the state government and Victorian universities that is being built in Parkville, with the diminutive title that contemporary institutions feel compelled to coin. The university itself is part of a national alliance, the Group of Eight, as the country's leading research universities press their distinctive interests.

These and other mechanisms facilitate the work of the University as it reaches its sesquicentenary. Those who work within it sometimes feel their operation as a benefit and sometimes as a burden. A centralised timetable allows rational use of scarce resources, but those who learn that their lecture is to be given at a distant theatre and too late in the week to follow it with tutorials see this as just one more tribulation. The university has always been a cumbrous institution composed of intensely intelligent and stubbornly independent individuals, strongly attached to the ways of their particular discipline; the academic vocation depends on the capacity of teachers and researcher to make their own judgements. If those charged with leading the university sometimes despair of its protean nature, their plethora of plans and targets, incentives and disincentives risks becoming the lightning-rod of resentment. Today's university is a semi-public corporation, increasingly reliant on contracts and customers to make good the deficiencies of public provision; it is more independent of government and yet more dependent on commercial forces beyond its control.

Both academic and administrative staff feel the pressure. Research undertaken by the Centre for the Study of Higher Education revealed that they work longer hours and feel less satisfaction—as student enrolments increase while staff numbers remain stable. The 4500 new international students recruited since 1996 have paid for salary increases and improvement of the physical fabric of the university, and they have enriched university life. But they have not allowed for a corresponding number of additional staff—they represent what one professor described at the Academic Board as 'sweat equity'. The enterprise agreement concluded in 2001 after long negotiation with the union, and several cases of industrial action, indicated the strain.

The improvements in teaching and assessment, the development of multimedia, the achievements in research, the efforts to achieve greater gender equity and inclusiveness, the better mentoring of novitiates and the greater cultivation of external relations all require greater effort, more co-ordination, additional committees and meetings. Even the program to assist heads perform their time-consuming tasks calls for additional time. Few academics can indulge in the long and alcoholic lunches at University House that were a feature of a more leisurely age.

Some of the impositions are particularly damaging to morale because they operate in a peremptory manner that emphasises the loss of autonomy. The body that funds medical research required that its recipients observe ethical standards. The university therefore established an ethics committee. The ambit was then extended to all researchers, regardless of discipline, as a condition of that body's grants, so that scholars in the social sciences and humanities were required to conform to its code. Postgraduate and even undergraduate students had to obtain prior approval of the appropriateness of their investigations into subjects far removed from medical experimentation and methodologies that are just as different. No one would dispute the need for ethical practice but some would question the ethical basis of this regulatory aggrandisement.

The survivors of the more relaxed era perhaps feel the loss most strongly for the expectations they brought to their career are at sharp variance with the altered regimen. They find the brisker, more businesslike atmosphere uncongenial and tend to take the benefits for granted—improved amenities, more research opportunities, generous provision for study leave, conferences and international partnerships. There is no shortage of applicants for vacancies and the younger members of staff bring a more realistic enthusiasm. They are more likely to have had outside work experience, less likely to expect to remain where they are until retirement. They are more adaptable, more familiar and comfortable with change as a constant. The efforts to sustain collegiality, which remains a strong feature at Melbourne, owe much to the university's officers and especially the Senior Vice-Principal, Ian Marshman, who has done much to break down the separation of academic from administrative staff. The liveliness or torpor of proceedings at Academic Board provide an index of the state of morale.

The students feel similar pressures. Most of them have to fit in their studies around many hours of paid employment. They are able to express their judgements on the university's teaching and support services, but find their teachers less accessible for informal contact. They expect high standards, for some have paid large fees and others are accumulating a significant debt through the deferred payment scheme. Their parents are anxious about their future prospects, their careers advisors have fed them with information about employment rates and salaries. For all the stress on vocational outcomes, the students display a remarkable intellectual curiosity.

Student life in the 1990s: the plain fare in the congested Caf gave way to small groups of more discriminating consumers in the court outside the Union. (courtesy Rick de Carteret)

Many find the transition from school to university a daunting challenge: you move from an academy on an intimate scale where no one is a stranger to a large, anonymous campus where few faces are the same from one class to the next and your companions seem dauntingly confident. There is alarming evidence of students who return to their lodgings between classes, and who have still to learn how to use the library well into first year. As Melbourne has increased its prestige and the breadth of its intake, rural students and those who have managed to obtain a place from unfashionable government or Catholic schools find the atmosphere increasingly intimidating. The university allocates a proportion of its places on the basis of equity, and provides scholarship support according to means, but the need to knit students into a community is as great as when Raymond Priestley arrived.

◊ ◊ ◊

The young Geoffrey Blainey completed his centenary history of the University of Melbourne with an appraisal of its achievement. He noted the slow growth of a colonial foundation into a large, diverse and vigorous academic institution. As the university grew, however, it acquired characteristics far removed from its founders' intentions. The growing professional and technological slant worried those who tended the pure flame of learning, but gave the university its strength and influence. The increase of knowledge brought a greater specialisation that 'tended to disintegrate the university', yet the increased emphasis on research was accompanied by greater intellectual freedom. A greater measure of self-government tended to deprive the university of community engagement in its affairs, while 'university policy on important issues has been removed from the realm of effective democratic discussion not only amongst the overwhelming majority of graduates, but also among the majority of the university's staff'. Blainey suggested that this lack of involvement explained the apathy of former students: 'In effect, the university asks them for their money but not for their intellect'.

Some of the changes that he saw after the university's first hundred years are still apparent; others have been overtaken by subsequent transformations. The further growth of the professions and dramatic expansion of research are now bound far more closely into the knowledge economy. Its need for knowledge workers who combine highly specialised expertise with a breadth of understanding creates new linkages in teaching, and the need to renew knowledge extends the contact of many students with the university well beyond their first degree. Research is conducted by teams and in centres across traditional disciplinary boundaries and far closer to its end-users. The self-government of the university was reduced by the expansion of Commonwealth involvement in tertiary education, then strengthened to make good Canberra's failure. Democracy waxed and waned. Fees were lifted, then reimposed.

The separation of the university from its community that Blainey regretted is apparent in the desultory character of public discussion. Melbourne

How Worldly?

Orientation week in the early 1990s: the student clubs and societies set up stalls on the Concrete Lawn to recruit the newcomers. (courtesy Rick de Carteret)

clamours with other universities for media attention to its activities, yet higher education policy has operated over the past decade in a remarkable vacuum. We hear of the country's universities when a scandal breaks, yet repeated appeals for greater support from vice-chancellors, staff and student unions, professional and business organisations, fall on deaf Canberra ears. For both major political parties this is a high-cost, high-risk issue best treated with platitudes. Within its own community, the University of Melbourne attracts intense scrutiny from the *Age*, whose writers and readers share a proprietorial interest in the fortunes of their *alma mater*. Whenever the *Age* reports a departure of the university from its accepted mission, the denunciation finds an eager response. Whenever the newspaper seeks to explain the departure, it betrays a credulous incomprehension of the academic enterprise. The need for those who constitute the university to explain its logic and values to those who care about its fortunes has never been greater.

Perhaps the most disturbing aspect of the new order is its impermanency. Universities are now managed, not governed, and management means constant improvement. This university was created to affirm the cultural continuity of a young colony with a distant parent society. Its first buildings recreated a traditional academic setting on wasteland. Its degrees, its academic dress, customs and rituals preserve these links. It is indeed an old university, second only to Sydney in Australian seniority and older than the overwhelming majority of universities throughout the world. It has only recently become a university of world standing, after a process of adaptation that started almost as soon as it began. Its first Chancellor, Redmond Barry, chose as its motto a classical phrase, *Postera crescam laude*, to proclaim that Melbourne would grow in the esteem of future generations. The greatest of all its obligations is to posterity.

Acknowledgements

R. J. W. Selleck's *The Shop* (2003), covering the first eighty years of the University of Melbourne, complements the earlier work of John Poynter and Carolyn Rasmussen, *A Place Apart*, which covered the subsequent sixty years. Together they provide a detailed history of its activity. This short history is offered to readers whose curiosity has been stimulated by the university's sesquicentennial celebrations. A short history is necessarily selective and we have selected those aspects and themes that have shaped the university over the past 150 years. Selleck prepared the first two chapters and Macintyre the last two, to a common plan and with full collaboration. A list of sources is appended for those seeking further guidance.

Stuart Macintyre has drawn on Geoffrey Blainey's centenary history of the university and a number of faculty and departmental histories. He owes a particular debt to John Poynter and Carolyn Rasmussen for their remarkably informative study, *A Place Apart*, and also for their generosity in allowing him to incorporate the fruits of their research into his chapters. Mention should also be made of the History of the University Project, funded by the Vice-Chancellor and directed until recently by Don Garden, which has supported, aired and published much useful research. Simon Booth, Christina Buckridge, Diana Bell, Amirah Inglis and Keir Reeves assisted with pictorial research. Frank Bongiorno, Tom Healy, Ken Inglis, Craig McInnis, Peter McPhee, Ray Marginson, Ian Marshman, Jim Mitchell, Rob Pascoe, John

Acknowledgements

Poynter, Carolyn Rasmussen, Helen Vorrath, Ross Williams and David Wood provided additional information and helpful advice.

Richard Selleck would like also to acknowledge a debt to Geoffrey Blainey's centenary history, to *A Place Apart* and to the History of the University Project, especially Don Garden. Mrs Poonam Mehra of Property and Building assisted both authors in the choice of illustrations. He owes special debts to the University of Melbourne Archives (particularly Liz Agostino), the Centre for the Study of Higher Education, Viv Kelly, Colin Goodwin, Peter McPhee and Margaret Pawsey.

Unless otherwise attributed in the captions, all illustrations are reproduced by courtesy of the University of Melbourne Archives. The State Library of Victoria; Trinity College at the University of Melbourne; the National Archives, New South Wales; and the Mathieson Library, Monash University have waived reproduction fees for the illustrations obtained from them.

Stuart Macintyre

R. J. W. Selleck

Editorial note

Abbreviations

ANU	Australian National University
ARC	Australian Research Council
ASIO	Australian Security and Intelligence Organisation
CRTS	Commonwealth Reconstruction Training Scheme
CSIR	Council for Scientific and Industrial Research
CSIRO	Commonwealth Scientific and Industrial Research Organisation
DEET	Department of Employment, Education and Training
EFTSU	Equivalent Full-Time Student Unit
MEI	Melbourne Enterprises International
MUM	*Melbourne University Magazine*
SDS	Students for a Democratic Society
SRC	Students' Representative Council
TAFE	Technical and Further Education

Illustrations

Unless otherwise attributed in the captions, all illustrations are reproduced by courtesy of the University of Melbourne Archives.

Chancellors and Vice-Chancellors

Chancellors

Sir Redmond Barry, 17 May 1853 to 23 November 1880
Sir William Foster Stawell, 2 May 1881 to 8th May 1882
The Rt. Rev. Dr James Moorhouse, 7 July 1884 to 1 February 1886
Dr William Edward Hearn, 3 May to 4 October 1886
Sir Anthony Colling Brownless, 4 April 1887 to 3 December 1897
Sir John Madden, 20 December 1897 to 10 March 1918
Sir John Henry MacFarland, 8 April 1918 to 22 July 1935
Sir James William Barrett, 30 August 1935 to 6 March 1939
Sir John Greig Latham, 6 March 1939 to 3 March 1941
Sir Charles John Lowe, 3 March 1941 to March 1954
Sir Arthur Dean, 15 March 1954 to 7 March 1966
Sir William George Dismore Upjohn, 7 March 1966 to 6 March 1967
Sir Robert Gordon Menzies, 6 March 1967 to 6 March 1972
Leonard William Weickhardt, 6 March 1972 to 18 March 1978
Sir Oliver James Gillard, 18 March 1978 to 3 March 1980
Sir Roy Douglas Wright, 3 March 1980 to 31 December 1989
Sir (Albert) Edward Woodward, 1 January 1990 to 2 February 2001
Fay Surtees Marles, from 2 February 2001

Vice-Chancellors

Honorary

Hugh Cullin Eardley Childers, 17 May 1853 to 12 March 1857
William Clark Haines, 15 May 1857 to 31 May 1858
Sir Anthony Colling Brownless, 31 May 1858 to 4 April 1887
Martin Howy Irving, 2 May 1887 to 27 May 1889
Sir John Madden, 3 June 1889 to 20 December 1897
Sir Henry John Wrixon, 20 December 1897 to 7 March 1910
Sir John Henry MacFarland, 7 March 1910 to 8 April 1918
Sir John Grice, 6 May 1918 to 18 June 1923
Sir John Monash, 2 July 1923 to 8 October 1931
Sir James William Barrett, 7 December 1931 to 17 December 1934

Salaried

Sir Raymond Edward Priestley, 1 January 1935 to 30 June 1938
Sir John Dudley Gibbs Medley, 1 July 1938 to 1 July 1951
Sir George Whitecross Paton, 1 July 1951 to 29 February 1968
Sir David Plumley Derham, 1 March 1968 to 31 May 1982
Professor David Edmund Caro, 1 June 1982 to 31 December 1987
Professor David Geoffrey Penington, 1 January 1988 to 31 December 1995
Professor Alan David Gilbert, from 1 January 1996

Sources

Australian Dictionary of Biography, Melbourne University Press, 1966– .

Colin Robert Badger, *Who Was Badger?*, Council of Adult Education, Melbourne, 1984.

Geoffrey Blainey, *A Centenary History of the University of Melbourne*, Melbourne University Press, 1957.

Robert Blake, *Disraeli*, Eyre and Spottiswoode, London, 1966.

Nicholas Brown, *Governing Prosperity*, Cambridge University Press, Melbourne, 1995.

Vincent Buckley, *Cutting Green Hay*, Penguin, Melbourne, 1983.

Ruth Campbell, *A History of the Melbourne Law School*, Faculty of Law, University of Melbourne, 1977.

M. A. Clements, The Co-ordination of Professional Training in Victoria, 1895–1905, with particular reference to the role of the secondary schools, M.Ed. thesis, University of Melbourne, 1974.

J. R. Darling, *Richly Rewarding*, Hill of Content / Lloyd O'Neil, Melbourne, 1978.

Hume Dow (ed.), *Memories of Melbourne University* and *More Memories of Melbourne University*, Hutchinson of Australia, Melbourne, 1983 and 1985.

Sue Ebury, *Weary: the life of Sir Edward Dunlop*, Viking, Melbourne, 1994.

S. G. Foster and Margaret M. Varghese, *The Making of the Australian National University 1946–1996*, Allen & Unwin, Sydney, 1996.

Ann Galbally, *Redmond Barry*, Melbourne University Press, 1995.

Lawrence M. Geary, 'Australian medical students in 19th century Scotland', *Proceedings of the Royal College of Physicians, Edinburgh*, vol. 26, 1996.

Philip Goad and George Tibbits, *Architecture on Campus: a guide to the buildings of the University of Melbourne and its residential colleges,* Melbourne University Press, 2003.

Sources

Patricia Grimshaw and Lynne Strahan (eds), *The Half-Open Door*, Hale and Iremonger, Sydney, 1982.

L. R. Humphreys, *Wadham*, Melbourne University Press, 2000.

Barry Humphries, *More Please*, Penguin, Melbourne, 1992.

Farley Kelly, *Degrees of Liberation: a short history of women in the University of Melbourne*, Women Graduates Centenary Committee of the University of Melbourne, 1985.

Graham Little, *The University Experience*, Melbourne University Press, 1970.

K. A. Lodewycks, *The Funding of Wisdom*, Spectrum, Melbourne, 1982.

Stuart Macintyre, *A History for a Nation*: *Ernest Scott and the making of Australian history*, Melbourne University Press, 1994.

——*The Oxford History of Australia: the succeeding age, 1901–1942*, Oxford University Press, Melbourne, 1993.

David S. Macmillan, *Australian Universities*, Sydney University Press, 1968.

Peter McPhee, *'Pansy': a life of Roy Douglas Wright*, Melbourne University Press, 1999.

Simon Marginson, *Educating Australia*, Cambridge University Press, Melbourne, 1997.

—— *Remaking the University: Monash*, Allen & Unwin, Sydney, 2000.

John Mulvaney, Howard Morphy and Alison Petch (eds), *My Dear Spencer: the letters of F. J. Gillen to Baldwin Spencer*, Hyland House, Melbourne, 1997.

P. W. Musgrave, *From Humanity to Utility: Melbourne University and public examinations, 1856–1964*, Australian Council for Educational Research, Melbourne, 1992.

Patrick O'Farrell, *UNSW, A Portrait*, University of New South Wales Press, Sydney, 1999.

John Poynter and Carolyn Rasmussen, *A Place Apart, the University of Melbourne: Decades of Challenge*, Melbourne University Press, 1996.

Raymond Priestley, *The Diary of a Vice-Chancellor*, edited by Ronald Ridley, Melbourne University Press, 2002.

Sheldon Rothblatt, *The Modern University and its Discontents*, Cambridge University Press, 1997.

Ernest Scott, *A History of the University of Melbourne*, Melbourne University Press, 1936.

R. J. W. Selleck, *The 'Shop': The University of Melbourne, 1850–1939*, Melbourne University Press, 2003.

Geoffrey Serle, *Sir John Medley*, Melbourne University Press, 1993.

Christopher Stray, *Classics Transformed: Schools, Universities, and Society in England, 1830–1960*, Clarendon Press, Oxford, 1998.

Marjorie Theobald, *Knowing Women: Origins of Women's Education in Nineteenth-Century Australia*, Cambridge University Press, 1996.

Sources

George Tibbits, *The Planning and Development of the University of Melbourne*, History of the University Unit, University of Melbourne, 2000.

T. G. Tucker, *Things Worth Thinking About*, E. W. Cole, Melbourne, 1910.

Clifford Turney and others (vol. 1) and W. F. Connell and others (vol. 2), *Australia's First: a history of the University of Sydney,* Hale and Iremonger, Sydney, 1991 and 1995.

Len Weickhardt, *Masson of Melbourne*, Royal Australian Chemical Institute, Melbourne, 1989.

Fay Woodhouse, A Place Apart? a study of student engagement at the University of Melbourne 1930–1939, Ph.D. thesis, University of Melbourne, 2001.

Victoria Worstead 'A profile of Bella Guerin, Australia's first woman graduate', *Victorian Historical Journal*, vol. 53, nos 2 and 3, 1982.

Index

Index

Index

Index